The T&T Clark Hebrew Primer

The T&T Clark Hebrew Primer

For Revision and Consolidation

A.A. Macintosh

&

C.L. Engle

B L O O M S B U R Y

LONDON • NEW DELHI • NEW YORK • SYDNEY

Bloomsbury T&T Clark
An imprint of Bloomsbury Publishing Plc

50 Bedford Square
London
WC1B 3DP
UK

1385 Broadway
New York
NY 10018
USA

www.bloomsbury.com

Bloomsbury is a registered trade mark of Bloomsbury Publishing Plc

First published 2014

British Library Cataloguing-in-Publication Data
A catalogue record for this book is available from the British Library.

ISBN:	HB:	978-0-56704-237-8
	PB:	978-0-56745-657-1
	ePDF:	978-0-56719-733-7

Library of Congress Cataloging-in-Publication Data
A.A. Macintosh and C.L. Engle
Hebrew Primer/ A.A. Macintosh and C.L. Engle
p.cm
Includes bibliographic references and index.
ISBN 978-0-567-04237-8 (hardcover)

Typeset by Forthcoming Publications (www.forthpub.com)
Printed and bound in Great Britain

Contents

Preface

The primer is, as its title suggests, designed to facilitate revision and consolidation for those who are following, or who have followed, the standard courses of instruction in elementary Hebrew, as also for those who, after an interval of neglect, wish to revive their knowledge of the language and their ability to read the Hebrew Bible.

The need for such a primer has become apparent to A.A.M. who has taught elementary Hebrew in the University of Cambridge for some forty years. It is apparent also to C.L.E. who, when charged with teaching the language for the first time, found herself reaching for just such a complementary teaching aid. It is hoped, then, that the primer will be of use to students as they follow their own particular courses of instruction and as they revise for examinations. In this connection it is important to note that the work is not allied to a particular teaching grammar but, rather, is designed to complement any and all such grammars. It is essentially a companion to the teaching grammars which seeks to give an additional perspective to their contents.

Most modern teaching grammars tend to submit the material to their readers with minimal exposition of a number of the fundamental principles which may be said to govern the language. It has become unfashionable, for example, to use descriptions familiar from the classical languages, such as declensions and conjugations. Indeed, it is noticeable that contemporary students, quite unfamiliar with such terms, show resistance to adopting them. The primer seeks in a gentle way to redress this tendency by rehearsing a number of the fundamental principles. Examples include the a/e vowel shift so typical of Hebrew, and categories of nouns (*sic* in this work) which, once grasped, have extended relevance to the entire verbal system.

A vocabulary consisting of words most frequently in use in the Hebrew Bible has been supplied. To particular words information ('gossip') has been added in order both to aid memory and to indicate connections in various aspects of Hebrew and its Semitic context. This includes some references to the modern spoken form of the language in Israel, now so vigorously successful. Such pieces of information undoubtedly arouse interest and consequent facility in learning.

The primer has been described by a colleague as 'a poor man's Gesenius Kautzsch'. If it is such, we shall be well pleased. It is, however, important to note that it is not fully comprehensive, and that not everything which could have been (or indeed, perhaps, in some cases should have been) included has been. The aim has been to review what would seem to be absolutely essential—what can speedily and in a manageable way be digested in revision and consolidation, and is also free from modern linguistic jargon.

We are immensely grateful to our colleagues H.G.M. Williamson and R.P. Gordon for their kindness in reading drafts of the work. Any mistakes and infelicities that survive are those of the authors and emphatically not at all those of the learned Professors. We wish also to thank Emily Brown for technical assistance, and Michelle Hunt for valuable suggestions.

It is a pleasure to acknowledge our indebtedness to A.B. Davidson's *An Introductory Hebrew Grammar*, first published by T. & T. Clark in 1874, and to the edition revised by Mauchline in 1962. We wish to thank Dominic Mattos of Bloomsbury T&T Clark, who graciously supported the idea of the primer. The work of Duncan Burns, our Senior Copy-Editor, has been exemplary, and we are deeply grateful to him for his patience and perseverance in bringing the work to completion.

A.A.M.   C.L.E.

Introduction

Vowel Signs
Vowel signs used in this Primer are listed in English for convenience as follows:

Patach	short a	◌
Seghol	short e	◌
Hireq	short i	◌
Qibbutz	short u	◌
Qametz-Hatuph	short o	◌
Qametz	long a	◌
Tsere	long e as in (s)ay	◌
Shureq	long u	ו
Holem	long o	◌
Shewa	Indistinct vowel	◌

The *hatephs*, or composite, directional *shewas* are: ◌ ◌ ◌ ("o" direction). These each denote a sound leaning in the direction of the corresponding short vowel. The terms are used interchangeably throughout this Primer.

Pure long vowels are: ◌י and ◌י as in "see" and "they", respectively
ו and ו as in "mow" and "rule", respectively

An illustration of Hebrew "a" vowels, using the vowel sounds of the English word "dance":

American = d*a*nce "ă" as in "cat"; equivalent to Hebrew *patach*
British = d*ah*nce "ah" as in "father"; equivalent to Hebrew *qametz*
French = d*a*nse "aw" as in "awning, awesome", or "daughter"; equivalent to Hebrew *qametz-hatuph*; cf., also, the English pronunciation of "bottle"

1

Dagesh forte indicates a doubled consonant. The associated vowel point belongs to the second occurrence, the first occurrence having an implicit silent *shewa*; e.g., בִּקֵּשׁ (*biqqesh*).

Dagesh lene is found only in the letters בגדכפת (*begadkephat*) when they begin a word or when they follow a silent *shewa* within a word; e.g., תִּכְתֹּב (*tiktob*).

The a/e Shift

This is a very common phenomenon in Hebrew and (spoken) Arabic. For example, the article in Arabic is ʾal-, but is very frequently pronounced ʾel-; cf. the place names ʾel-Alamein and ʾel-medinah. In Hebrew the tendency likewise occurs both in verbs and in nouns. "a" vowels shift to "e" vowels, as also do "i" vowels.

The shift occurs in nouns—מַלְכָּה "queen", but מֶלֶךְ "king" (a/e shift); סִפְרָה "book", but סֵפֶר "book" (i/e shift)—and verbs: imperfects in "a" in very common verbs display the same tendency (for further explanation, see **2f**, **3a**, and **3b** below).

    Examples: נָתַן "to give", imf יִתֵּן > יִתַּן
                        יָרַד "to go down", יֵרֵד > יֵרַד

Open and Closed Syllables

An open syllable consists of a consonant followed by a vowel; a closed consists of consonant–vowel–consonant.

Feminine Endings

The *old* feminine ending in both Hebrew and Arabic is ת.
    Examples: יְהוּדִית "Judith, Jewish woman"; *bint* (Arabic) = בַּת "daughter"

The *new* and most common feminine ending is הָ (*qametz-he*), found in many girl's names.
    Examples: Deborah, Susannah, Hannah and Sarah

The *old* feminine ending reappears:

1. in construct forms, when these are combined with following absolutes;
2. when suffixes are added to *new* feminine forms (in both nouns and 3fs verbal forms).

Examples:

1.   שָׂפָה "lip" >   שְׂפַת־הַמֶּלֶךְ "lip of the king", "the king's lip"

                                שְׂפַת־הַיָּם "lip of the sea", "seashore"

                                שְׂפָתַיִם "(two) lips"

2.   אָכְלָה "she ate" >   אֲכָלָתְהוּ "she/it ate him" (Gen. 37:33)

Stress

Indications of stress (accents) are provided in this Primer as an aid where it is important to do so.

Unattested Forms

In the interests of expedience and the facility of learning, a number of forms which are not attested in the Hebrew Bible have been deployed; e.g., the recitation of the *Qal* imperfect of קטל as an imperfect in "a", parallel to its proper recitation as an imperfect in "o".

1

Nouns and Adjectives

1a. Nouns and Adjectives

Nouns and adjectives in Hebrew may be grouped into six categories. Of these, *the first three are crucially important*, and attention to them will enable the reader to master a large number of Hebrew nouns (and adjectives), as well as the forms of the verbal system. The categories, sometimes called declensions, may be labelled and described as follows:

First Category. Identification: one or more ָ (*qametz*) must be present, excluding the *qametz* of the feminine ending.

 Examples: זָקֵן רָצוֹן פָּקִיד גָּדוֹל דָּבָר

Second Category. Identification: one or more ֶ (*seghol*), and occasionally two ַ (*patach*).

 Examples: נַעַר זֶרַע קֹדֶשׁ סֵפֶר מֶלֶךְ

Third Category. Identification: negatively, not first or second category; positively, having in the first syllable a pure long vowel or short vowel in a closed syllable, with ֵ (*tsere*) in the second syllable.

 Examples: כֹּהֵן מוֹעֵד מִזְבֵּחַ קוֹטֵל

Fourth Category. Nouns with a medial (middle) ו (*waw*) or י (*yod*), and two syllables. They may, for convenience, be described as "collapsers", since, when suffixes are added, or when in the construct singular form, they are reduced from two syllables to one.

5

Examples: מָוֶת > מוֹת (cstr)

בַּיִת > בֵּית (cstr)

תָּוֶךְ > תּוֹךְ–

מוֹתוֹ "his death" (with suffix, attached to the collapsed form)

בֵּיתִי "my house" (with suffix, attached to the collapsed form)

Fifth Category. This category comprises nouns (a) derived from roots whose third radical is ה or י; (b) nouns in which the second and third radicals are the same, but are written only once (hence, they are usually monosyllables). For convenience, the latter may be described as "doublers". Since both these groups are very closely related to verbal forms with the same characteristics, it is convenient to set them out in association with those verbs. See (a) under III-*He/lamed-he* verbs, **3d**, and (b) under Geminate/double *ayin* verbs, **3fa** below.

Sixth Category. Negatively, none of the above; positively, nouns having *shewa* in the first syllable, and nouns in which all the syllables are by nature unchangeable. Here, since there are never internal vowel changes (either in the construct form or with the addition of syllables), they are described for convenience as "no change nouns".

Examples: חֲלוֹם בְּרִית אֱלֹהִים

1b. First Category
The stress in this category falls upon the last syllable. When nouns (and adjectives) with two syllables increase to three syllables, the *qametz* of the first syllable always reduces to a sounded *shewa*. This principle has been called the "see-saw", in that the heavier ending reduces the weight of the initial syllable. If the initial consonant is a guttural, then the *shewa* is a *hateph* (directional or composite *shewa*). The second syllable remains unaltered.

Examples: דְּבָרוֹ דְּבָרִים > דָּבָר

חֲכָמִים > חָכָם

גְּדוֹלִים > גָּדוֹל

רְצוֹנִי > רָצוֹן

Construct forms have a *patach* in the second (closed) syllable, and the first (open) syllable reduces to *shewa*. If a guttural is the first letter, then the *shewa* is a *hateph.*

Examples: דְּבַר⁻ > דָּבָר

עֲפַר⁻ > עָפָר

If the first or second syllable has a pure long vowel (*waw* or *yod*), this is unchangeable.

Examples: כּוֹכַב⁻ > כּוֹכָב

פָּקִיד⁻ > פָּקִיד

Similarly, a short (closed) first syllable is unchangeable. *Note*: an unstressed closed syllable MUST have a short vowel.

Example: מִכְתַּב⁻ > מִכְתָּב

Construct plural forms: the masculine ending ◌ִים becomes ◌ֵי as universally. The second syllable, being open, reduces to sounded *shewa*. The resulting form with two sounded, adjacent *shewas* is *prohibited*, and the first *shewa* becomes *hireq* to avoid the problem.

Example: דְּבָרִים (absolute) > דְּבְרֵי⁻ (*prohibited*) > דִּבְרֵי⁻ (construct)

If the first consonant is a guttural, *hireq* is replaced with the full vowel of the *hateph* (directional *shewa*) of the absolute plural.

Example: חַכְמֵי⁻ > חֲכָמִים

1b*a*. A variant form of the First Category occurs with a relatively small number of words, e.g., גָּמָל "camel" or קָטָן/קָטֹן "small". The first syllable reduces to *shewa* as normally, but the second syllable becomes a *patach* (or corresponding short vowel) before a doubled third radical.

Examples: גָּמָל "camel" > גְּמַלִּים (pl)

קָטָן "small" > קְטַנִּים (pl)

עָמֹק "deep" > עֲמֻקִּים (pl)

The plural constructs display no change, apart from the ending, since the vowels have become unchangeable.

1b*b*. Feminine Nouns

These, with the ־ָה ending added, are already three syllable words. Consequently, the initial syllable is already a sounded *shewa*. If the word lengthens by the addition of suffixes, the second syllable becomes (sounded) *shewa*, and the resulting two *shewas* require *hireq* or *patach* in the initial syllable. Compare masculine nouns above.

Examples: צְדָקָה "righteousness" > צִדְקָתִי "my righteousness"

נְבֵלָה "corpse" > נִבְלָתָהּ "her corpse"

אֲדָמָה "ground" > אַדְמָתוֹ "his ground"; here *patach*, the full vowel of the *hateph* rather than *hireq*

בְּרָכָה "blessing" > בִּרְכַּת־ "blessing of" (exceptionally with silent *shewa*)

1bc. Suffixes

The rules listed above apply to the addition of suffixes, i.e., when two syllables become three, or when three become four (feminine nouns). The only variation is that the heavy suffixes (כֶם– כֶן– הֶם– הֶן–) are *always preceded by construct forms*. Note, also, that the suffix ־ֶךָ counts as a single syllable.

Examples: (ms) דָּבָר "word" > דְּבָרוֹ "his word", דְּבָרָהּ "her word"

BUT   דְּבַרְכֶם "your word"

(fs) צְדָקָה "righteousness" > צִדְקָתוֹ "his righteousness",

צִדְקָתֵנוּ "our righteousness"

BUT   צִדְקַתְכֶם "your righteousness"

(mpl) דְּבָרִים > דְּבָרֶיךָ, דְּבָרַיִךְ

BUT   דִּבְרֵיכֶם

(fpl) צִדְקוֹת > צִדְקוֹתַי and צִדְקוֹתֵיכֶם

1b*d*. Some Important Prepositions of the First Category

"Before" is expressed in Hebrew by the preposition לְ and the noun פָּנִים "face". This latter is a plural noun, and the two syllables already include the plural ending. Consequently, there is no third syllable and, therefore, no call for a *shewa* in the first syllable. When suffixes are added, the First Category rules apply, and the construct plural form is used before the heavy suffixes, and *before these only*. It is a very common mistake to use the construct form before all the suffixes.

Examples: לְפָנִים (pl abs + לְ) > ־לִפְנֵי (cstr) "before (any noun)"

לְפָנַי "before me"

לְפָנֶיךָ "before you"

לְפָנֶיהָ "before her"

BUT   לִפְנֵיכֶם (so also ־הֵן – הֶם– כֶן–)

־עַל "upon". This is a First Category monosyllable, and like פָּנִים it is plural in form. With suffixes, the first syllable becomes an open *qametz* throughout, *except for the heavy suffixes* which require the construct form, the latter using a *hateph* because of the guttural עׂ.

Examples: עָלִים (theoretical) absolute

־עֲלֵי (cstr)

עָלָיו "upon him"

עָלֶיהָ "upon her"

BUT   עֲלֵיכֶם "upon you" (mpl); cf. the famous greeting שָׁלוֹם עֲלֵיכֶם

[אֶל] ־אֶל "unto" (*seghol* with hyphen only; with *tsere* only when part of a word). This is also a First Category monosyllable. The *tsere* (rather than the older *patach/qametz*) represents an example of the widespread a/e shift (see a/e shift in the Introduction, above). The preposition behaves exactly as ־עַל above, except that *tsere* replaces the original *patach/qametz*. The forms with heavy suffixes have an "a" class *hateph*, an indication that the original vowel was "a" rather than "e".

Examples: אֵלֶיךָ "to you" (ms)

אֵלַיִךְ "to you" (fs)

אֵלָיו "to him"

BUT   אֲלֵיהֶם "to them" (mpl)

1b*e*. Verbal Forms

The First Category also provides the model for vowel changes in the perfect *Qal* when suffixes are added. Imperfects in "a" also follow this rule. The resulting forms must conform to the familiar collocation of three syllables as in דְּבָרִים (from דָּבָר).

Examples: קָטַל "he killed" > קְטָלוֹ "he killed him"

> קְטָלַנִי "he killed me" (stress on the –לַ–)

> קְטַלְתַּנִי "you killed me" (stress on the –תַּ–); cf. Jesus' cry from the cross *sabachthani* "you have forsaken me" (Mark 15:34; Aramaic form)

יִשְׁמַע "he will hear" > יִשְׁמָעֵנִי "he will hear me"

> יִשְׁמָעֵהוּ "he will hear him"

See further under Verbal Suffixes in **2g** below.

The passive participle of the *Qal* also conforms to the First Category.

Example: שָׁאוּל "asked for" > שְׁאוּלָה (fs)

1c. Second Category

All Second Category nouns have the stress on the first syllable; contrast the First Category where the stress falls on the last syllable. Second Category nouns show evidence of vowel shift, i.e., the ubiquitous a/e shift, as well as an i/e shift. If we take the word for "queen" מַלְכָּה, and compare it with the word for "king" מֶלֶךְ, we can deduce that מַלְכָּה retains the older ground form (the "a" vowel), and that מֶלֶךְ has evolved from מַלְךְ. The first step is that the cluster of consonants at the end of the word is separated by the insertion of an "e" vowel, resulting in מַלֶךְ.[1] The second stage is that the first vowel is subject to the a/e shift, resulting in the full

---

1. A parallel may be seen in Greek πέτρος, which becomes "Peter" in English, thereby breaking up the cluster of consonants in the middle of the word. In colloquial American English the word "athlete" is sometimes pronounced ath-uh-leet, following exactly the same principle.

segholate form מֶלֶךְ. It should be noted that this *segholate* form is restricted to the absolute and the construct singular, and does not appear elsewhere. This constitutes class (a) of the Second Category nouns.

A second class (b) has the ground form סִפְּר which follows a similar development. First, the *seghol* separates the cluster of consonants (under פ and ר) resulting in סֵפֶר and, secondly, a subsequent i/e shift (under the ס) results in סֵפֶר "book".

A third class (c) has the ground form בָּקְר (with *qametz-hatuph*; cf. the sound of English "bottle", or American "long", or in both languages "ought, daughter, awning", these preserving an "*aw*" sound) which follows the pattern of the (a) and (b) classes: > בָּקֶר and then, instead of a vowel shift in the first syllable, there is a lengthening of the "o" vowel to *holem*, resulting in the form בֹּקֶר "morning".

The construct singular of all three classes is the same as the absolute.

1c*a*. Singular

When Second Category two-syllable nouns increase by the addition of suffixes (or gender or number endings), the ground form of each of the three classes is resumed in: the *singular*, the *dual*,[2] the *construct plural*, and the *plural* with *heavy suffixes* (–ֶהן –ָכן ֶהם– –ָכם).

> Examples: (a class) מַלְכֵיכֶם מַלְכֵי⁻ מַלְכִים מַלְכִי מֶלֶךְ
> (b class) סִפְרֵיכֶם סִפְרֵי⁻ סְפָרִים סֵפֶר
> (c class) בָּקְרֵיהֶן בָּקְרֵי⁻ בְּקָרִים בָּקְרָה בֹּקֶר (◌ָ is *qametz-hatuph*)

Note: Where the second radical of these original forms has *shewa*, in the singular (all forms) and dual (all forms) it is silent, but in the plural it is sounded (see **1c*b*** below).

2. The *dual* is used mainly for natural pairs, e.g., feet, hands.

1c*b*. Plural

The plural forms of *all* these nouns are identical to the plurals of the First Category (e.g., דְּבָרִים, see **1b** above).

Examples: מְלָכִים > מֶלֶךְ

סְפָרִים > סֵפֶר

בְּקָרִים > בֹּקֶר[3]

When suffixes are added to the plural forms (other than the construct and the heavy suffix forms) the rules are identical to those of First Category plurals (see **1b** above).

Generally speaking, nouns with one or two *seghols* have מַלְךְ as their ground form, but some such nouns (particularly those having a *tsere* in the first place) have סְפֶר as their ground form.

Nouns with a guttural as *third* radical have *patach* in the second position, always. This indicates that the guttural has preserved the older "a" vowel, preventing the a/e shift.

Examples: זֶרַע "seed"; the ground form is זַרְעְ

מֶלַח "salt"; the ground form is מַלְחָ[4]

Nouns with a guttural as *second* radical do not entertain any *seghol*. This indicates that the guttural in second position has required the retention of two "a" vowels, always *patach*, again preventing the a/e shift.

Example: נַעַר "boy"; the ground form is נַעְרָ

---

3.   *Note*: the plural forms of some class (c) nouns have a *hateph* (an "o" directional *shewa*), rather than a simple *shewa* and, again, some forms have a *qametz-hatuph*; cf. חֳדָשִׁים, and קֳדָשִׁים (קֳ is *qametz-hatuph*).

4.   Cf. and contrast, also, מֶלַח "salt" and מֶלֶךְ "king", where the ח in מֶלַח preserves the "a" vowel which precedes it. See further under יָם "sea", in the Vocabulary.

1cc. Feminine Nouns with Second Category Endings

Examples of these are מַמְלָכָת "kingdom", קוֹהֶלָת "preacher" ("Ecclesiastes"), מֵינֶקֶת "nurse". These nouns retain the first syllable unchanged, and the remaining parts of the words behave exactly as the masculine nouns above, with the stress on the first *segholate* syllable.

Examples: מַמְלַכְתִּי "my kingdom"

קוֹהַלְתֵּנוּ "our preacher" (not found in the Bible)

מֵינִקְתֵּךְ "your nurse"

1cd. An Important Second Category Form

The *Qal* infinitive construct/verbal noun of the regular verb, having the form קְטוֹל/קְטֹל, is a (disguised) Second Category noun of the (c) class. Its ground form is קָטְל (*qametz-hatuph*; cf. the sound of English "bottle"), and it is to this form that suffixes are attached.

Examples: קָטְל > קָטְלִי "my killing" (i.e., "I am doing the killing", subjective suffix), see also **2d** below

> קָטְלֵנִי "my killing" ("I am being killed", an objective suffix)

> קָטְלְכֶם "your killing" (subjective and objective)

Other than the first person suffix, forms of the infinitive construct/verbal noun do not differentiate between subjective and objective suffixes, and the context dictates which is meant.

1d. Third Category

The most obvious example of a Third Category noun is the active participle of the *Qal*. The form can be written קֹטֵל or קוֹטֵל; hereafter, in this Primer, both forms are used interchangeably. A second group in the Third Category have a short, closed syllable in first position. In either case, when the word becomes three syllables rather than two, the first syllable always remains unaltered. The second syllable always reduces to a sounded *shewa*. If the medial letter is a guttural, the *shewa* becomes a *hateph*.

Examples: קֹטֵל < קֹטְלִים or קֹטְלוֹת (participle forms)

כֹּהֵן < כֹּהֲנִים "priest(s)"

מִזְבֵּחַ < מִזְבְּחִי "altar, my altar"

There is only one complication, and that arises from the ־ְךָ suffix, with its sounded *shewa*.

    Example: קֹטֵל "killer" > קֹטְלְךָ "your killer" BUT two sounded *shewas* together are *prohibited*; therefore the form becomes קֹטֶלְךָ, the (full vowel) *seghol* replacing the first of the *shewas*.

1da. The Feminine

The feminine form of קוֹטֵל may be קוֹטְלָה, in accordance with what has already been explained in **1d** above. The much more common feminine form, however, uses the old feminine ת ending.

    Example: קוֹטֶלֶת (cf. קוֹהֶלֶת *Qohelet* = Ecclesiastes "the convener/preacher")

Note: if the root has a guttural letter in second or third place, the underlying "a" vowels do not undergo the a/e shift; e.g., פּוֹרַחַת in Gen. 40:10. Compare the principle explained in **1cb** above. It will be apparent, further, that these forms have migrated to that of a Second Category feminine, or *segholate* noun, the rules for which have been set out in **1cc** above.

1db. Important Third Category Forms

It is helpful to note that **all** *Niphals*, *Piels*, and *Puals*, as well as imperfect *Qal* forms with "o" as the last vowel, approximate to Third Category nouns. The first syllable is usually closed and short.

    Examples: יִקְטֹל < יִקְטְלוּ (*Qal* imf in "o")

                נִקְטַל < נִקְטְלוּ (*Niphal* pf)

                קִטֵּל < קִטְּלָה (*Piel* pf)

                יְקַטֵּל < יְקַטְּלוּ (*Piel* imf)

In the fourth example (יְקַטְּלוּ) there are four syllables, rather than three. The first contains the unalterable *shewa* of the *Piel*, and the second syllable (–קַטְּ–) corresponds to the first, unalterable syllable of the Third Category (here a closed, short syllable).

1e. Fourth Category

Nouns in this class have a weak middle radical, a *waw* or a *yod*. When any modification is made to two-syllable nouns of this category, they "collapse" into one syllable. Others have already "collapsed", and no further modification is necessary.

Examples: בַּיִת "house" > בֵּית־ "house of" (cstr), בֵּיתוֹ "his house"⁵

זַיִת "olive" > הַזֵּיתִים (הַר־) (Mt. of) Olives

מָוֶת "death" > מוֹתְךָ "your death", מוֹתָהּ "her death"

קוֹל "voice" > קוֹלִי "my voice", קוֹלֵנוּ "our voice"⁶

אֵיד "disaster" > אֵידְכֶם "your (pl) disaster"

In this category there are one or two cases where the plural reverts to two syllables:

Example: חַיִל "strength" (cf. the famous אֵשֶׁת־חַיִל "woman of strength, character", Prov. 31:10); the plural form is not חֵילִים as expected, but חֲיָלִים "strengths, armies", First Category form.

1f. Fifth Category

1fa. Examples of nouns from III-*He*/*lamed-he* roots are:

1. These have retained their original י: חֲלִי פְּרִי אֲרִי

2. In these, the ה has replaced the י: יָפֶה שָׂדֶה מִשְׁתֶּה יָפָה (fem), where the ה is that of the feminine ending, because the י / ה of the root has thus been "burnt off", eliminated.

---

5. This very common word has an irregular plural form; one would expect בֵּיתִים, but in fact the plural is בָּתִּים.

6. Hebrew often uses the singular for parts of the body predicated of a plural entity; for example, *all* the people have *one* voice, *one* heart.

1fb. Examples of nouns from Geminate/double *ayin* roots, almost always monosyllables:

עַם (from עמם)	עַמִּים (pl)
הַר (from הרר)	הָרִים (pl)
חֹק (from חקק)	חֻקִּים (pl)
צֵל (from צלל)	צִלּוֹ "his shadow"

For the rules governing **1fa**, see **3de**; for **1fb**, see **3fa**.

1g. Sixth Category

This category is the simplest of all. There are no internal changes to the vowels when two syllables become three or more.

Examples:

בְּרִית "covenant" >	בְּרִיתִי "my covenant"
אֱלֹהִים "God" >	אֱלֹהֵי־ "God of"
	אֱלֹהַי "my God" (the plural ending expressing majesty/greatness)
חֲלוֹם "dream" >	חֲלֹמוֹ "his dream"
	חֲלֹמוֹת "dreams" (mpl with, unusually, a morphologically fpl ending)
מַרְעִיף (*Hiphil* ptc) "trickling, dripping" >	מַרְעִיפִים (mpl) "trickling, dripping (of clouds)"

2

Strong Verbs

Note: the following general considerations should be considered:

1. The forms and endings in all verbs and all themes of the verb are, without exception, identical. It is *imperative to memorize completely* the basic perfect and imperfect forms of the *Qal*.

2. Grammarians of Semitic languages use the third masculine singular (3ms) form to represent the verb, because it is the simplest form. Second and first person forms follow in that order.

2a. Perfect Form of the *Qal*

The perfect form of the simple verb (*Qal*) may be grouped in the pattern 3-2-1-2-1 for easy rhythmic recitation as follows:

קָטַל	"he killed"		קָטְלוּ	"they killed"
קָטְלָה	"she killed"			
קָטַלְתָּ	"you (ms) killed"		קְטַלְתֶּם	"you (mpl) killed"
			קְטַלְתֶּן	"you (fpl) killed"
קָטַלְתְּ	"you (fs) killed"			
קָטַלְתִּי	"I killed"		קָטַלְנוּ	"we killed"

Note: the two second plural forms reduce the first syllable to *shewa*, because the תֶּם– תֶּן– endings are heavy. The *Qal* is the only theme (or stem) of the verb in which this occurs.

17

2b. Imperfect Form of the *Qal*

There are *four* initial closed syllables for the *Qal* imperfect: יִקְ– תִּקְ– אֶקְ– נִקְ–

This consonantal pattern, י–‎ ת–‎ א–‎ and נ–, applies to imperfects of ALL other verbs and themes.

> The imperfect form of the simple verb (*Qal*) is grouped in the pattern 3-2-4-1, again for easy rhythmic recitation:
>
> | | | | |
> |---|---|---|---|
> | יִקְטֹל | "he will kill" | יִקְטְלוּ | "they will kill" (mpl) |
> | תִּקְטֹל | "she will kill" | תִּקְטֹלְנָה | "they will kill" (fpl) |
> | תִּקְטֹל | "you will kill" (ms) | תִּקְטְלוּ | "you (all) will kill" (mpl) |
> | | | תִּקְטֹלְנָה | "you (all) will kill" (fpl) |
> | תִּקְטְלִי | "you will kill" (fs) | | |
> | אֶקְטֹל | "I shall kill" | נִקְטֹל | "we shall kill" |
>
> For imperfects with "a" vowel rather than "o" in the last place (named 'imperfects in "a"'), see **2f** and **3g**.

2c. The Participle

There are two participles of the *Qal*, active and passive. They are, respectively, קוֹטֵל (cf. כֹּהֵן "priest") and קָטוּל (cf. בָּרוּךְ *Baruch*, Jeremiah's scribe, "Blessed"). The active participle is a Third Category noun/adjective, and the passive a First Category. For details, see above under Nouns, **1d** and **1b**, respectively. For the common feminine form קוֹטֶלֶת using the old feminine ending, see under Nouns, **1cc** and **1da** above.

2d. The Imperative and Verbal Noun/Infinitive Construct

These are both formed by removing the תִּ– element from the beginning of the imperfect second person forms. Beginning with the imperative form:

Examples: תִּקְטֹל "you will kill" > קְטֹל "kill!" (the silent *shewa* of the imperfect now becoming sounded in an open syllable)

תִּקְטְלוּ‎ "you will kill!" (mpl) > קְטְלוּ‎ > קִטְלוּ‎

(Removal of the ‎תְּ‎ results in a prohibited form with two sounded *shewas* together; consequently, the first shewa is changed to *hireq*.)

The 2ms imperative behaves as a Second Category (c) noun/adjective (with *qametz-hatuph*) when suffixes are added to it.

Examples: קָטְלֵנִי‎ "kill me!"   קָטְלֵהוּ‎ "kill him!"

The other imperative forms are Sixth Category with no change.

2da. The verbal noun/infinitive construct is formed in the same way.

Examples: קְטֹל‎ or קְטוֹל‎ (as in "killing is forbidden") and לִקְטֹל‎ (as in "to kill is forbidden"; here, the sounded *shewa* becomes silent in the resulting closed syllable).

When suffixes are applied to the verbal noun it behaves as a Second Category (c) noun/adjective.

Examples (all forms with *qametz-hatuph*):

קָטְלֵנִי‎ "my killing" (= "I am being killed")

קָטְלִי‎ "my killing" (= "I am doing the killing"); this distinction between objective and subjective suffix applies only to the first person. So קָטְלוֹ‎ means "his killing" (regardless of whether he is killed or is doing the killing).

The other forms of the imperative belong to the Sixth Category nouns/adjectives, and there is no change when suffixes are added.

The two crucial signposts for the *Qal*: יִקְטֹל קָטַל‎

2e. The Seven Themes of the Verb
I. *Qal* or Simple Form (set out above)
II. *Niphal* Reflexive/Passive
III. *Piel* Intensive/Factitive/Causative
IV. *Pual* Intensive/Passive
V. *Hiphil* Causative/Internal (Demonstrative)
VI. *Hophal* Causative/Passive
VII. *Hithpael* Reflexive/Self-Performance (of *Piel*)

It should be noted that few, if any, verbs make use of all these themes in the Hebrew Bible.

2ea. *Niphal*
The perfect has the short, initial closed syllable –קְנִ throughout. The endings are as in the *Qal* above.

Examples: נִקְטַל נִקְטַלְתִּי נִקְטְלוּ

The imperfect has the initial short, closed syllable –קִּיִ. The four initial syllables (here two) of the tense in this theme are thus: –קִּיִ –קִּתִ –קִּאֶ or –קִּאַ and –קִּנִ. The endings are as above, though the final syllable is in ◌ֵ when nothing follows.

Examples: יִקָּטֵל תִּקָּטְלִי יִקָּטְלוּ תִּקָּטַלְנָה

The *dagesh forte* in קּ represents an assimilation of the original *Niphal* נ, as in –קִּיִ > –קְנִיִ.

The ◌ְלֹ endings in the imperfect (when nothing follows the third radical) represent a shift from a probable original "i" vowel.

The meaning of the *Niphal* is properly reflexive, but it is most commonly used as a passive. Thus it may mean either "he was killed" or "he killed himself".

Participle

The participle of the *Niphal* is of the form נִקְטָל and it belongs to First Category nouns/adjectives, but with a closed, unalterable first syllable.

Examples: נִקְטָלָה נִקְטָלִים

Imperative and Verbal Noun/Infinitive Construct

The imperative is formed by removing the –תִ element from the beginning of the imperfect second person forms. Since the following first radical is doubled, and cannot start a word, –הִ is imported to begin the word.

Examples: הִקָּטֵל הִקָּטְלוּ

The verbal noun/infinitive construct is also הִקָּטֵל. It behaves like Third Category nouns/adjectives when suffixes are added; e.g., הִקָּטְלוֹ "his being killed".

> **The two crucial signposts for the *Niphal*:** יִקָּטֵל נִקְטַל.

2eb. Piel

The middle radical is doubled throughout this theme, as well as in the *Pual* and the *Hithpael*. The perfect uses an "i" vowel in the initial closed syllable (i.e., –קִטּ throughout). The endings are as in the *Qal*, see **2a** above.

Examples: קִטֵּל קִטְּלָה קִטְּלוּ קִטַּלְתִּי

The imperfect has a sounded *shewa* throughout in its initial syllable, which gives rise to the four initial combinations: –יְ, –תְ, –אֲ (*hateph* by reason of the guttural *aleph*) –נְ, and (ptc) –מְ. The vowel of the first radical is ◌ֵ instead of the ◌ַ of the perfect. The endings are as in the *Qal* above.

Examples: יְקַטֵּל תְּקַטְּלִי תְּקַטְּלוּ תְּקַטֵּלְנָה

Notes: The –◌ֵל endings in perfect and imperfect (i.e., when nothing follows the third radical) represent an a/e shift (which does not occur in the less used *Pual*). The original ◌ַ "a" vowel reappears in the perfect (and sometimes in the imperfect) when there are consonantal endings.

For the omission of *dagesh forte* in –ְיַ– following *waw* consecutive, see **5b** below.

A possible mnemonic for remembering the vowel of the first radical of perfect and imperfect *Piel* is: קְט־קַט ("kit-kat").

The basic meanings of the *Piel* are:
    intensive: i.e., to busy oneself eagerly with the action; from *Qal* "he killed" comes *Piel* "he massacred, he obliterated";
    causative: "he caused to kill";
    factitive: to name, describe or establish something as fact; cf., קִדֵּשׁ "he sanctified, made holy", here, with no a/e shift.

The Participle
In this theme, and in all themes except *Qal* and *Niphal*, the participle begins with –מְ. The *Piel* participle is formed by replacing the initial imperfect syllable –יְ with –מְ.
    Example: מְקַטֵּל (cf. מְנַחֵם "Menachem"). The form behaves in accordance with Third Category nouns/adjectives, e.g., מְקַטְּלִים.

The Imperative and Verbal Noun/Infinitive Construct
As usual, these are formed by removing the –תְ element from the beginning of the imperfect second person forms. The imperatives belong to Third Category nouns/adjectives, e.g., קַטֵּל קַטְּלוּ. Note the very familiar "Hallelujah": thus תְהַלֵּל > הַלֵּל > הַלְלוּ־יָהּ (for the omission of *dagesh forte* in this form, see **5b** below).

The verbal noun/infinitive construct is also קַטֵּל and behaves in accordance with Third Category nouns.

Associated with the *Piel* are nouns formed according to the קַטָּל / *qattāl* pattern, which denotes occupation.

Examples: גַּנָּב "thief"

טַבָּח "cook" (so also in Arabic)

מַלָּח "sailor"

דַּיָּן "judge"

צַלָּם "photographer" (Modern Hebrew).

> **The two crucial signposts for the *Piel*: יְקַטֵּל קִטֵּל**

2ec. *Pual*

The middle radical of the root is doubled throughout this theme. The vowel of the first radical is a short ◌ֻ forming the initial closed syllable קֻטַּ– throughout. The endings are as in the *Qal* above.

Examples: קֻטַּל קֻטַּלְתִּי קֻטְּלוּ

The imperfect also has the short ◌ֻ vowel in its first (root) position with doubled middle radical.

The four initial syllables are as in the *Piel*:

–יְ –תְּ –אֲ (*hateph* by reason of the guttural aleph) –נְ and (ptc) –מְ

Examples: תְּקֻטַּלְנָה תְּקֻטְּלוּ יְקֻטַּל

Note: The *Pual* theme is an easy one, though is not greatly used.

The meaning is the passive of the *Piel*: קֻטַּל "he was massacred".

Participle
The participle is formed by replacing the initial imperfect syllable –יְ with –מְ. It belongs to Third Category nouns/adjectives.

Examples: מְקֻטָּל מְקֻטָּלִים

Infinitive construct/verbal noun is, as expected, קֻטַּל following removal of the initial –תְּ.

Imperative does not occur in this theme.

> **The two crucial signposts for the *Pual*: יְקֻטַּל קֻטַּל**

2ed. *Hiphil*

–הִ is prefixed to the root, giving in the perfect an unalterable first closed syllable –הִקְ. The endings are as above in the *Qal*, EXCEPT that, with vowel endings and no endings, –יִ◌– is inserted between the second and third radicals. These forms are הִקְטִיל הִקְטִילָה הִקְטִילוּ.

Examples for the remainder: הִקְטַלְתָּ הִקְטַלְתֶּם הִקְטַלְנוּ

The imperfect has the four initial syllables as follows: –יַ –תַּ –אַ –נַ and (ptc) –מַ

All forms, except the feminine plurals, insert –יִ◌– before the third radical.

Examples: יַקְטִיל תַּקְטִיל תַּקְטִילִי יַקְטִילוּ

The only forms which have consonantal endings are the two feminine plural –נָה endings. Here, the vowel before the third radical has an a/e shift, from an original ◌; hence תַּקְטֵלְנָה.

Notes: The *Hiphil* is perhaps the most complicated theme of the verb, by reason of the insertion, or lack of insertion, of the –יִ◌– vowel.

In the jussive forms of the imperfect, and with *waw* consecutive, the forms that end with the third radical shorten from ◌ִיל to ◌ֵל (for other occurrences of this, see **3ca, 3d**). If anything occurs after the third radical, the long ◌ִיל– resumes its place. The first person with *waw* consecutive also retains the ◌ִי–: וָאַקְטִיל

Examples: תַּקְטֵל (jussive)

וַיַּקְטֵל

BUT וַיַּקְטִילוּ

The meaning of the *Hiphil* is causative, declaratory, or internal (the display of a tendency or characteristic).

Examples: הִקְטִיל "he caused to kill" (root קטל)

הִצְדִּיק "he declared innocent" (root צדק "be righteous")

הִשְׂכַּלְתִּי "I have displayed insight" (internal, root שׂכל; Ps. 119:99)

Participle

The participle is formed by replacing the –יַ element of the imperfect with –מַ. The resulting form belongs to Sixth Category nouns/adjectives where no change ensues.

Examples: מַקְטִילִים מַקְטִילָה

Imperative and Verbal Noun/Infinitive Construct

Somewhat like the *Niphal* imperative, –הַ replaces the initial –תַ element of the second person imperfect.

Examples: הַקְטֵל הַקְטִילוּ הַקְטֵלְנָה

Note: the *short* form ending of the 2ms imperfect is used, but the *long* form is used with vowel endings and suffixes. In other words, when anything comes after the last (third) radical, the long form reappears in all forms except, with its consonantal ending, הַקְטֵלְנָה.

The verbal noun/infinitive construct takes the form הַקְטִיל. It, too, belongs to Sixth Category nouns/adjectives where no change ensues.

> ### The crucial signposts of the *Hiphil*: הִקְטִיל יַקְטִיל (וַיַּקְטֵל)

2ee. Hophal

–הָ is prefixed to the root in the perfect, making an unalterable first syllable הָקְ–. The vowel is the short *qametz-hatuph*; cf. English "hot" or "bottle", or American "long", or in both languages "ought, daughter, awning" (with an "*aw*" sound). The remaining syllables are as in the *Qal*.

> The imperfect has its four initial syllables: –יָקְ, –תָּקְ, אָקְ, –נָקְ and (ptc) –מָקְ

Note: This theme is an easy one, though it is not greatly used.

The *Hophal* functions as the passive of the *Hiphil*, thus, "he was made to kill".

Participle

The participle is formed by replacing the –יָ element of the imperfect with –מָ. The form is מָקְטָל (the second *qametz* is the regular long "a" vowel), which belongs to First Category nouns/adjectives.

Imperative and Verbal Noun/Infinitive Construct

The imperative and verbal noun/infinitive construct do not occur in this theme.

> ### The crucial signposts of the *Hophal*: יָקְטַל הָקְטַל

2ef. Hithpael

–הִתְ is prefixed to the root in the perfect, making an unalterable first syllable. The collocation of vowels which follow –הִתְ is similar in form to the *Piel* theme.

Examples: הִתְקַטֵּל הִתְקַטְּלוּ הִתְקַטַּלְתֶּם

The imperfect has the four initial syllables: יִתָ– תִתָ– אֶתָ– נִתָ– and (ptc) מִתָ–

    Examples: תִּתְקַטְּלוּ אֶתְקַטֵּל תִּתְקַטְּלִי יִתְקַטֵּל

Notes: If the verb has a sibilant (ס צ שׂ שׁ) as first radical, metathesis occurs, i.e., the ת of the initial syllable and the sibilant change places. When צ is involved, the ת also hardens to ט.

    Examples: הִצְטַדֵּק תִּשְׁתַּמְּרוּ הִשְׁתַּמֵּר

The meaning of the *Hithpael* is formally and most often reflexive; sometimes it expresses an aspect of behaviour relating to the self. It includes "to show oneself as….", "to claim oneself to be…" (i.e., performing the action of the verb).

    Example: הִתְקַטֵּל "he killed himself"

In order to show the range of meaning in the *Hithpael*, and the flexibility of the verbal system, a more complete example is based on the root קָדַשׁ "to be holy":

        קָדַשׁ (*Qal*)   "to be holy"

        קִדֵּשׁ (*Piel*)   "to sanctify" (causative)

        הִתְקַדֵּשׁ (*Hithpael*) "he sanctified himself, he kept himself holy"

                                     "he consecrated himself" (of priests, Levites)

                                     "he caused himself to be hallowed" (of God)

Participle

The participle is formed by replacing the יִתָ– element of the imperfect with מִתָ–.

    Example: מִתְקַטֵּל, which belongs to Third Category nouns/adjectives, e.g., מִתְקַטְּלִים.

Imperative and Verbal Noun/Infinitive Construct

The imperative is formed by replacing the second person תָ– element of the imperfect with הָ–; thus, תִתָ– becomes הִתָ–, and the second ת does not change.

    Examples: הִתְקַטֵּלְנָה הִתְקַטְּלוּ הִתְקַטֵּל

הִתְקַטֵּל belongs to Third Category nouns/adjectives, and the other three forms of the imperative to Sixth Category.

The verbal noun/infinitive construct is also הִתְקַטֵּל and behaves in accordance with Third Category nouns/adjectives.

Notes: The 3ms pf form is the *same* as the 2ms imv and inf cstr: הִתְקַטֵּל
             The 3mpl pf form is the *same* as 2mpl imv: הִתְקַטְּלוּ

> **The crucial signposts of the *Hithpael*: יִתְקַטֵּל הִתְקַטֵּל**

2f. Stative Verbs

Stative verbs correspond loosely with intransitive verbs, but this description is not exhaustive. They are capable of denoting the condition of the subject, and therefore can sometimes be transitive, e.g., "to love", "to fear", "to know", as well as intransitive, "to be full", "to be thirsty", "to be hungry", "to be old", "to be big", etc. The perfect of the Stative verb is capable of a present meaning; e.g., יָדַעְתִּי גֹּאֲלִי חַי "I know that my Redeemer lives" (Job 19:25).

There are two types of Stative verb: the "a" type, and the "o" type. The only significant differences are found in the *Qal*.

Rules: ALL imperfects of Stative verbs, whether "a" type or "o", have imperfects in "a": (using קטל for convenience as a "teaching tool") תִּקְטְלוּ תִּקְטַל יִקְטַל, etc. This is to say that, where there is an "o" vowel in the regular *Qal* imperfect (see under **2b** above), it is here replaced by an "a" vowel, the remaining forms of the imperfect being the same as in the ordinary *Qal*.

"a" type verbs vary in the perfect ONLY by a *tendency* to have an "e" vowel in the 3ms instead of the regular "a" vowel; e.g., כָּבֵד "he was/is heavy", but קָדַשׁ "he was/is holy", keeping the regular "a" vowel. The WHOLE of the rest of the perfect is totally regular (see *Qal* **2a** above): כְּבָדְתֶּם כָּבְדוּ כָּבַדְתִּי

"o" type Stative verbs vary in the perfect in that the "a" vowels of the regular *Qal* perfect are replaced with "o" vowels; e.g., קָטֹן קָטֹנְתָּ קְטָנְתֶּם (here, –טָ– with *qametz-hatuph*). קָטְנוּ is identical to the regular verb, the "o" vowel, like the "a" in the regular verb, having already been reduced to *shewa*.

"o" type Stative verbs are few in number overall, though יָכֹל "he was/is able", occurs frequently. As has been stated, the imperfect of these verbs is in "a", e.g., יִקְטַן.

Note also יוּכַל (the imperfect of יָכֹל) with its unique long וּ.
    Examples: נוּכַל יוּכְלוּ תּוּכְלִי יוּכַל

The four initial syllables for this verb are, uniquely: נוּ– אוּ– תּוּ– יוּ–

Note: There is a certain symmetry here, in that the regular verb *Qal* has "a" vowels in the perfect, and "o" vowels in the imperfect; "o" type Statives do the reverse, having "o" vowels in the perfect and "a" vowels in the imperfect.

Participle
The participle of the Stative verb has a *qametz* instead of *holem*. Contrast the participle of the strong verb קֹטֵל "killer", with that of Stative verbs ("a" type) כָּבֵד "heavy, honourable", and ("o" type) קָטֹן "little". The Stative participles belong to First Category nouns/adjectives.

Imperative and Verbal Noun/Infinitive Construct
The imperative is formed exactly as in the strong verb. The vowel of the second syllable follows that of the imperfect.
    Example: כְּבַד "be heavy!"

In כְּבְדוּ (2mpl) the resulting form with two sounded *shewas* together is *prohibited*, and the first of them becomes *hireq*, thus > כִּבְדוּ; cf. כִּבְדִי (2fs).

The verbal noun/infinitive construct is formed by removing the first element of the imperfect as in the strong verb.

Examples: כְּבַד, but כְּבֹד is also found

> **The crucial signposts for Stative verbs are:**
> ("a" type) יִכְבַּד כָּבֵד
> ("o" type) יִקְטַן קָטֹן BUT uniquely (יָכֹל) יוּכַל

2g. Verbal Suffixes

> The object suffixes added to verbal forms are as follows:
>
> | | |
> |---|---|
> | וֹ– or וֹהוּ– "him" | ◌ם– "them" (m) |
> | ◌ָהּ– or (less common) ◌ָהָ– "her" | ן– "them" (f) |
> | ◌ְךָ– "you" (ms) | (2mpl does not occur) |
> | ◌ֵךְ– "you" (fs) | (2fpl does not occur) |
> | ◌ִי– "me" | נוּ– "us" |

Vowel Attachments
These are not needed when the verbal forms before the suffix end in a vowel.

Example: הִקְטִילוּנִי "they caused me to kill" (*Hiphil* pf 3cpl + 1cs suffix)

Generally speaking, *perfects* use an "a" connecting vowel when the verbal form ends in a consonant, whereas *imperfects* use an "e" vowel.

Examples: הִקְטִילָנוּ "he caused us to kill" (*Hiphil* pf 3ms + 1cpl suffix)
קְטָלַנִי "he has killed me" (*Qal* pf 3ms + 1cs suffix)
יַקְטִילֵנוּ "he will cause us to kill" (*Hiphil* imf 3ms + 1cpl suffix)

The new 3fs perfect ending ◌ָה– reverts to the old –◌ַת– before suffixes.

Example: אָכְלָתוֹ < אָכְלָה "she/it has eaten him" (Gen. 37:33)

Note: The 2ms suffix ךָ– already has a connecting vowel in its sounded *shewa*, but the suffix counts as one syllable only. Problems arise when the ךָ– suffix is added to a Third Category noun form whose final syllable reduces to *shewa*. The result is the *prohibited* two sounded *shewas*.

    Example: (*Piel* inf cstr) קַטֵּל > קַטְּלְךָ (*prohibited*)

                                   > קַטֶּלְךָ (where a full "e" vowel replaces the first

                                             sounded *shewa*)

Rules: The active tenses allow verbal suffixes, and the passive tenses do not. Of the active tenses, the *Hiphil* is the easiest, the *Piel* next easiest, and the hardest is the *Qal*.

- **Hiphil forms** of the verb behave as Sixth Category nouns/adjectives. There are no internal vowel changes.

- **Piel, and Qal imperfect forms in "o"** behave as Third Category nouns/adjectives. This means that once a suffix is added to forms which end with the third radical of the root, the vowel of the second root letter reduces to *shewa*.

    Examples:

      Piel perfect and imperfect: קִטֵּל > קִטְּלוֹ

                                      יְקַטֵּל > יְקַטְּלֵנִי

                                      קִטַּלְתִּי > קִטַּלְתִּיהָ (this now Sixth Category)

      Qal imperfect in "o":   תִּקְטֹל > תִּקְטְלֵהוּ

- **Qal perfect forms, and Qal imperfect forms in "a"** conform to First Category nouns/adjectives. The sound pattern of דְּבָרִים (from דָּבָר) is imposed upon the verb before the suffix. Thus, a sounded *shewa* marks the syllable two places before the stressed syllable (cf. the "see-saw" of First Category, **1b**).

    Examples (pf):

      קָטַל > קְטָלַנִי (the stress is upon the –טַל and –לַנִ-, respectively)

קְטַלְתָּ > קְטַלְתַּנִי; cf. (Aramaic) *sabachthani* "Thou hast forsaken me" (Mark 15:34)

קְטָלוּ > קְטָלוּהָ (the stress is upon –לוּ and –לוּ–, respectively)

Examples (imf):

יִשְׁמֹר > יִשְׁמְרֵנִי (Third Category), but יִשְׁמַע > יִשְׁמָעֵנִי (First Category)

יִשְׁמְרוּ > יִשְׁמְרוּנִי (now Sixth Category), but יִשְׁמְעוּ > יִשְׁמָעוּנִי (First Category)

The forms יִשְׁמְרוּ and יִשְׁמְעוּ are apparently identical, but with the addition of suffixes the difference obtrudes.

- **Qal infinitive construct/verbal nouns**. The form קְטֹל/קְטוֹל is a disguised Second Category (c), see **1ca**. Its ground form (with *qametz-hatuph*) is קְטָל, and it is to *this* form that suffixes are added.

       Examples: קָטְלִי¹ קָטְלְךָ קָטְלוֹ

Note: A very common Hebrew construction is to use the infinitive construct/verbal noun following the prepositions בְּ and כְּ to convey a temporal sense; e.g., "as his keeping…", meaning "while he kept". Thus, "while he kept the sheep…" > …כְּשָׁמְרוֹ אֶת־הַצֹּאן.

---

1.   קָטְלִי means "my killing" (I am doing the killing); קָטְלֵנִי means "my killing" (I am being killed). This distinction between subjective and objective suffixes only occurs for 1cs forms.

3

Weak Verbs

The vast majority of Hebrew verbs are formed of three letters. The weak verbs were labelled by the early Jewish grammarians in terms of פָּעַל "to do" (cf. the familiar English "doing word" to describe the function of a verb). Thus, for example, a *pe-nun* verb (root נפל) is so called because, by reference to פָּעַל, its *pe* (initial letter) is a *nun*. Or, again, מֹשֶׁה is called a *lamed-he* verb because, by reference to פָּעַל, its *lamed* (third letter) is a *he*. A double *ayin* verb is so called because its *ayin* (second letter) is repeated in third place, as in the root הלל. The names of the themes of the verb are formed in the same way, see **2e** above.

It has become common, especially in North America, to describe Weak Verbs by reference to the numerical placement of the three radical letters of the verb: I-, II-, III-. One class of verbs having a weak letter in its first place is, accordingly, described as I-*Aleph*, I-*Yod*, I-*Nun*, or I-*Guttural*, etc. Another class are those verbs having a weak second letter, which are described in the same way: II-*Waw*, II-*Yod*,[1] II-*Guttural*, etc. A third class follows the same principle: III-*Aleph*, III-*He*, III-*Guttural*. Verbs whose second and third letters are the same (double *ayin*, above) are called Geminate verbs, from the Latin for "twins" *gemini*. In this Primer both terms are used, e.g., I-*Nun/pe-nun* verbs.

3a. I-*Nun/pe-nun* Verbs
Verbs whose first radical is *nun*. In this class there is a tendency for the weak *nun* to assimilate, or merge, with the letter which follows it when the *nun* comes at the end of a closed syllable. The principal themes in use for these verbs are the *Qal* and the *Hiphil*.

---

[1] But see **3e** below, and the preferred alternative title, "Hollow verbs".

33

Qal Perfect:

> is regular, the *nun* is retained and there is no variation.

Qal Imperfect (in "o"):

> from root נפל "to fall": יִפֹּל > יִנְפֹּל the *dagesh forte* acknowledges the erstwhile presence of a *nun*.[2] The remainder of the tense follows the normal imperfect pattern: יִפְּלִי אֶפֹּל יִפְּלוּ

Qal Imperfect (in "a"):

> from root נגש "to draw near": יִגַּשׁ > יִנְגַּשׁ, thereafter as above, an "a" vowel occurring where the "o" vowel occurred in the root נפל.

Imperative:

> imperfects in "a" generate a monosyllabic imperative following the normal pattern:
>
> > גַּשׁ > תִּגַּשׁ, etc.
>
> imperfects in "o" on the other hand, reinstate the *nun*:
>
> > נְפֹל > תִּפֹּל (*prohibited*) > נְפֹלוּ ; נְפֹל > תִּפְּלוּ > נְפְלוּ

Participles:

> do not drop their *nun* and are regular, and they follow Third Category principles: נֹפֵל נֹגֵשׁ

Infinitive Construct/Verbal Noun:

> of imperfects in "o" is regular: נְפֹל

> of imperfects in "a" does not reinstate the *nun*, and takes a form comparable to Second Category (a) nouns/adjectives, see section **1c** above. It compensates for the omission of *nun* by adding the (old) feminine ending ת–: (from נֶגֶשׁ (נָגַשׁ) יִגַּשׁ > גַּשׁ > גַּשְׁתְּ > גֶּשֶׁת. The infinitive construct is, then, גֶּשֶׁת, and with suffixes obeys the rules of Second Category (a), see **1c** above; e.g., גַּשְׁתִּי "my drawing near" (גִּשְׁתִּי is also found). The stress on Second Category nouns (without suffixes) is on the first syllable, so that when ל is added, being before the stress, it is pointed לְ, thus לָגֶשֶׁת (see **1c** above; also **6b** item 2c below).

---

[2] N.B. The *dagesh* in the original יִנְפֹּל is a *dagesh lene* present in a "*begadkephat*" letter which follows a silent *shewa*; the *dagesh forte* in יִפֹּל represents the assimilated *nun*.

Hiphil forms are as expected, with *nun* merged:

> perfect/imperfect:
>
> > יַגִּישׁ   הִגִּישׁ   יַ, etc.
>
> imperative:
>
> > הַגֵּשׁ (but, in accordance with the principles governing *Hiphils*, *yod* is reinstated with any addition following the third radical, e.g., הַגִּישׁוּ)
>
> infinitive construct:
>
> > הַגִּישׁ
>
> participle:
>
> > מַגִּישׁ
>
> These latter two forms are Sixth Category.

> **The crucial signposts for I-*Nun*/*pe-nun* verbs are:**
>
> (imperfect in "a")   גֶּשֶׁת גַּשׁ יִגַּשׁ נָגַשׁ
>
> (imperfect in "o")   נְפֹל נָפֹל יִפֹּל נָפַל

3a*a*. "Giving" and "Taking"

There are two very common verbs which belong to the I-*Nun*/*pe-nun* class: נָתַן "to give" naturally does so, but לָקַח "to take" (not a I-*Nun*/*pe-nun* verb) is unique in doing so also.

> Perfect of נָתַן:
>
> > The final *nun* of the root merges with *consonantal* endings, and its residual presence is marked by a *dagesh forte*.
> >
> > > Examples: נָתַתִּי נְתַתֶּם נָתַתָּ (1cpl)
> >
> > But נָתְנוּ (3cpl) and נָתְנָה with their *vowel* endings behave normally.
>
> Perfect of לָקַח: is normal.
>
> Imperfect of נָתַן: יִנְתַּן > יִתֵּן > יִתֵּן (with a/e shift); thus, e.g., יִתְּנוּ אֶתֵּן יִתֵּן
>
> Imperfect of לָקַח: יִלְקַח > יִקַּח; thus, e.g., תִּקַּחְנָה אֶקַּח
>
> Participles are regular: נֹתֵן and לֹקֵחַ (with furtive *patach*)

Imperatives: do not reinstate the first *nun/lamed*; e.g., קַח "take!" and תֵּן "give!"

Infinitive Construct/Verbal Noun: both verbs import the feminine ת– at the end of the word in compensation for the loss of the first radical.

> Examples: קָחַת > קַח > יִקַּח > לְקַח The infinitive construct is, thus, קַחַת, the guttural ח preventing the a/e shift: קַחַת קַחְתּוֹ לְקַחַת
>
> תֵּת > תֶּנֶת > תֶּנְתְּ > תֵּן > יִתֵּן > נָתַן In the infinitive construct תֵּת, considerably weakened, both radical *nuns* have disappeared. The form approximates to monosyllabic Second Category (b) noun/adjective, see **1c** above. With suffixes, תֵּת becomes –תִּתְ; e.g., תִּתִּי "my giving", תִּתְּךָ "your giving", etc. (the doubled, second ת marks the residual presence of a *nun*).

The crucial signposts for "giving" and "taking" are:

"*giving*" נָתַן: יִתֵּן (תֵּת –תִּתְ inf cstr)

"*taking*" לְקַח: יִקַּח (קַחַת inf cstr)

3b. I-*Yod(waw)/pe-yod(waw)* Verbs

Verbs whose initial letter is usually *yod* (הָלַךְ is the exception). The most important in this category are the six very common verbs set out as follows:

יָרַד	"to go down" (cf. יַרְדֵּן "Jordan")	יָלַד	"to bear"
יָצָא	"to go out" (יְצִיאָה "exit", Modern Hebrew)	יָשַׁב	"to sit, dwell"
הָלַךְ	"to walk, go" (cf. *Halakah* in Judaism)	יָדַע	"to know"

Note: Migration of Consonants. All six of these verbs originally had *waw* as their first radical. (It is useful here to compare the Hebrew words יֶלֶד "boy" and יַלְדָּה "girl" with Arabic *walad* "boy" and *waldah* "girl", where the true first radical is preserved in the Arabic.) In some forms of these six verbs the original *waw* reappears (see below). All the original *waws* have, over time, migrated to *yods* in the *Qal*. The extremely common verb הָלַךְ also clearly belongs to this class, and its initial ה represents a yet further migration of the first radical from *waw* through *yod* to *he*. (In the III-*He/lamed-he* verbs the third radical *yod* consistently migrates to *he* when it marks the end of a word; see **3d** below.) Another example of this migration is an original שָׂרָי > שָׂרָה, Abraham's wife; see further, **3d***a* below.

The *Qal* Perfect:

> of these verbs is entirely normal. *Yod* and, in the case of הָלַךְ, *he*, is the first consonant throughout.

>> Examples: יָצְאָתָם יָשְׁבוּ הָלַכְתִּי יָלַדְתָּ יָדַעְתָּ יָרְדָה   In this last case the final *aleph* of the root quiesces; see III-*Aleph/lamed-aleph* verbs, **3g***e* below.

Qal Participles are entirely regular:

> Examples: יֹשֵׁב "dweller"   יָלוּד "born"

Qal Imperfect:

> ALL six verbs, originally with imperfects in "a", drop the *yod* of the root throughout this tense, and adopt, by reason of the a/e shift, two *tseres* as vowels. יֵרֵד יֵלֵד יֵשֵׁב are quite straightforward; הָלַךְ יָצָא יָדַע are all subject to understandable minor variations.

>> Examples: יֵלֵךְ יֵרֵד (from הָלַךְ)
>> יֵדַע (note the *ayin* prevents the a/e shift)
>> יֵצֵא (note the quiescent *aleph*).

The other forms are normal: תֵּלַדְנָה יֵלְכוּ (note here that the –לַךְ– syllable does not succumb to the a/e shift).

The four initial syllables for these verbs are: –יֵ –תֵּ –אֵ –נֵ

Waw Consecutive and Retracted Tone:

> When *waw* consecutive is added to forms of the imperfect which end with the third radical (but NOT the 1cs form), there occurs a phenomenon known as the "retracted tone". For example, יֵשֵׁב has the stress on the last syllable; but וַיֵּשֶׁב has the stress on the –יֵּ– syllable, and that has the effect of shortening the final *tsere* into *seghol* in the unstressed, closed syllable שֶׁב–.

Imperative:

> The imperative is formed normally, and the –תִּ in the first syllable of the imperfect 2s and pl vanishes, resulting in forms:
>
> שְׂרוּ דַּע רַדְנָה לְדִי דְּעוּ שְׁבוּ לֵךְ רֵד צֵא

Verbal Noun/Infinitive Construct:

> The infinitive construct is formed by removing the first element of the imperfect and adding the (old) feminine ת– at the end of the word. (Hebrew does not like monosyllabic infinitives construct.)
>
> Examples (from יָשַׁב): (imf) יֵשֵׁב > שֶׁב > שֶׁבְתָּ > שֶׁבֶת
>
> The infinitive construct שֶׁבֶת behaves in accordance with Second Category (b) nouns/adjectives.

Examples:	שִׁבְתִּי	"my sitting"
BUT	דֵּעֹתוֹ	"his knowing"; the infinitive construct of יָדַע is דַּעַת, because the *ayin* has prevented any a/e shift.
	צֵאתְךָ	"your going out" (with quiescent *aleph*)
	לְדְתָּה	"her bearing"
	לֶכְתָּם	"their going"; note that here, this very common form has an i/e shift from an expected לִכְתָּם.

Hiphil:

> The very common six verbs, being originally I-*Waw*/*pe-waw*
> verbs, retain the original *waw* in the *Hiphil* perfect:
>
> הוֹלִיד > [3] הוֹלִיד (יֶלֶד from root) (from root יָלַד)
>
> The initial syllable of all forms of the *Hiphil* perfect is –הוֹ.
> In the imperfect the four initial syllables are: –יוֹ –תּוֹ –אוֹ –נוֹ
> and (ptc) –מוֹ

The endings of the *Hiphil* perfect, imperfect, participle and verbal noun/infinitive
construct are regular.

Examples (from root יָשַׁב):

> הוֹשַׁבְתֶּם הוֹשִׁיבוּ הוֹשִׁיב (perfect)
> יוֹשִׁיבוּ יוֹשִׁיב (imperfect)
> מוֹשִׁיב (participle) (Sixth Category nouns/adjectives, see **1g** above)
> הוֹשִׁיב (verbal noun/infinitive construct) (Sixth Category nouns/
> adjectives, see **1g** above)

The phenomenon of the retracted tone applies also to the *Hiphil* imperfect when
the word ends with the last radical (but NOT the 1cs form, which does not
shorten), e.g., יוֹשִׁיב; BUT with *waw* consecutive the short form וַיֹּשֶׁב > יֹשֵׁב
(see *Qal* above). *Note*: וַיּוֹשִׁיבוּ, where the full form resumes, because the word
does not end with the third radical.

Imperative. This behaves in a similar way: הוֹשֵׁב (2ms), BUT הוֹשִׁיבוּ (2mpl)

Niphal:

> The perfect takes the form נוֹלַד (from root יָלַד) where, again, the
> original *waw* reappears. The development is: נוֹלַד > נְוְלַד. The
> imperfect takes the form יִוָּלֵד; here the original *waw*, being
> doubled, is totally unalterable. Both perfect and imperfect are
> thereafter normal.

[3] By reference to Arabic, the first syllable is likely to have been –הֻו.

> **The crucial signposts for four of the six most common I-*Yod*(*waw*)/*pe-yod*(*waw*) verbs** are set out in full because of their importance:
>
> | ילד | *Qal*: לֶדֶת לֵד יֵלֵד יָלַד | *Hiphil*: הוֹלֵד וַיּוֹלֶד יוֹלִיד הוֹלִיד |
> | ישב | *Qal*: שֶׁבֶת שֵׁב יֵשֵׁב יָשַׁב | *Hiphil*: הוֹשֵׁב וַיּוֹשֶׁב יוֹשִׁיב הוֹשִׁיב |
> | ידע | *Qal*: דַּעַת דַּע יֵדַע יָדַע | *Hiphil*: הוֹדֵעַ וַיּוֹדַע יוֹדִיעַ הוֹדִיעַ |
> | יצא | *Qal*: צֵאת צֵא יֵצֵא יָצָא | *Hiphil*: הוֹצֵא וַיּוֹצֵא יוֹצִיא הוֹצִיא |

3c. I-*Yod*/*pe-yod* Verbs

Those whose initial letter was never *waw*, but always *yod*. This constitutes a subcategory, sometimes called "pure *pe-yod* verbs", in order to distinguish them from those verbs whose *yod* was originally a *waw* (**3b** above).

> *Qal* perfect:
>> is quite normal: יָרְשׁוּ יָרַשְׁתִּי יָרַשׁ
>
> *Qal* imperfect:
>> unlike **3b** above, it retains the *yod* of the root which, following *hireq*, becomes a pure long vowel: תִּירַשְׁנָה יִירְשׁוּ יִירַשׁ
>> The four initial syllables of the *Qal* imperfect are then: נִי– אִי– תִּי– יִי–
>
> Participles:
>> are entirely regular: יוֹנֵק "suckling" יָרוּשׁ "possessed"
>
> Imperative and the infinitive construct/verbal noun:
>> tend to drop the *yod* of the root, so:
>> רְשׁוּ and רַשׁ (imv)
>> רֶשֶׁת (inf cstr < רִשְׁתְּ; cf. שֶׁבֶת immediately above, **3b**)
>
> *Hiphil*:
>> Using the root ינק "to suck" (*Hiphil* "to suckle, nurse")
>> Perfect: is הֵינִיק (from הִינִיק, by dissimilation), where הֵי– is the first syllable throughout.

Imperfect: follows with its four forms: ‫יְ‑‬ ‫תִּי‑‬ ‫אִי‑‬ ‫נֵי‑‬ and (ptc) ‫מֵי‑‬
Imperatives: ‫הֵינַק הֵינִיקוּ‬
Forms with *waw* consecutive (retracted tone): ‫וַיֵּינַק‬, but as usual ‫וַיֵּינִיקוּ‬

Note: The common verb ‫יָרַשׁ‬ "to possess" is anomalous, in that it follows I-*Yod*/
pe-yod 3c pattern in the *Qal*, but the 3b pattern in the *Hiphil*.
    Examples: ‫יִירַשׁ‬, but ‫יוֹרִישׁ / הוֹרִישׁ‬

3d. III-*He*/*lamed-he* Verbs
3da. Perfects:
These verbs are cited in the 3ms with *qametz-he* at the end; e.g., ‫עָשָׂה‬ "to make/do"
or ‫גָּלָה‬ "to uncover, remove". The *he*, though, represents a migration from an
original *yod*, much as the I-*Yod*/*pe-yod* verb ‫הָלַךְ‬ "to walk/go" conceals an original
yod, ‫יָלַךְ‬. This phenomenon is exemplified by two words: the name ‫שָׂרָה‬ "Sarah" is
noted by Gen. 17:15 to have been originally ‫שָׂרַי‬ "Sarai".[4] Again the archaic form
of the word for "field" ‫שָׂדֶה‬ was ‫שָׂדַי‬. The *Qal* passive participle of these verbs ·
retains that original *yod*: ‫גָּלוּי עָשׂוּי‬ (First Category).

- The original *yod* reappears throughout ALL themes of these verbs, when
  the forms have a consonantal ending.
      Examples from root ‫עשׂה‬: ‫עָשִׂיתֶם עָשִׂיתִי‬
      from root ‫גלה‬: (*Niphal*) ‫נִגְלֵיתָ‬
      (*Piel*) ‫גִּלִּיתִי‬
      (*Hiphil*) ‫הִגְלֵיתֶם‬, etc.
- In the case of pure long vowel endings in all themes, the weak *he/yod*
  third radical ending is burnt off and disappears completely.
      Examples (as above): ‫הִגְלוּ גָּלוּ נִגְלוּ עָשׂוּ‬

---

[4] In fact, the ‫‑ִי‬ ending here is believed to be an ancient feminine, replaced by the new
feminine ‫‑ָה‬; the root of ‫שׂר‬ is, in any case, a geminate/double *ayin* and not III-*He*/*lamed-he*.
The phenomenon of this name change, however, witnesses to the principle of *yod* migrating to
he and serves as a useful mnemonic.

- In the 3fs ending the final radical is replaced with the old feminine ־ת־, and to that is added the new feminine ־ה.

Examples from עָשָׂה: עָשְׂתָה

from גָּלָה: (Niphal) נִגְלְתָה

3db. Imperfects:

The same rules apply:

- Before the only consonantal ending of the imperfect, ־נָה, the original *yod* reappears.
- Pure long vowel endings burn off the weak third radical.
- When nothing follows the third radical, it migrates to *he* as in the 3ms perfect cited above, but it is preceded by *seghol* in all themes of the verb.

Examples: יִגְלֶה תִּגְלֶה נִגְלֶה תִּגְלִי יִגְלוּ תִּגְלֶינָה יִגָּלֶה יִגְלֶה תִּגְלוּ, etc.

3dc.

> With these principles in mind, we may state that:
>
> ALL PERFECTS have as their initial signpost הָ־ *qametz-he*
>
> ALL IMPERFECTS have as their initial signpost הֶ־ *seghol-he*
>
> ALL PARTICIPLES have as their initial signpost הֶ־ *seghol-he*
>
> ALL IMPERATIVES have as their initial signpost הֵ־ *tsere-he*
>
> ALL VERBAL NOUNS/INFINITIVES CONSTRUCT have as
> their signpost ־וֹת *holem-waw-taw*.

The participles and imperatives behave according to the principles stated above, the elimination of the third radical being very common.

The verbal nouns/infinitives construct belong to Sixth Category nouns/adjectives.

Note: The vowel preceding the restored *yod* in active tenses is *hireq*, and in passive/reflexive tenses is *tsere*.

Examples: (Piel) גִּלִּיתָ (Niphal) נִגְלֵיתָ

3dd. Apocopated forms:

If III-*He*/*lamed-he* verbs are characterised by some consistency and facility, they compensate by having some rather complicated forms in connection with *waw consecutive*. We return here to the principle of the retracted tone. For example, יִגְלֶה has the stress on the last syllable –לֶה; but וַיִּגְלֶה has its stress on the –יִּ– syllable. The effect of this retraction is so to weaken the last syllable that it falls away and disappears. The resulting form is וַיִּגְל. This, being the original form of a Second Category (b) noun/adjective, manifests, sometimes partially, sometimes fully, the shift to *segholates* (i/e shift). The form then becomes וַיִּגֶל. *Hiphil* forms (see immediately below) manifest the Second Category (a) noun/adjective a/e shift. It should be noted that this phenomenon occurs ONLY when the last radical ends a word in its ה– form (i.e., in 2ms, 3ms and 3fs forms). It does NOT occur when the other natural verb endings are in place. The phenomenon occurs as follows:

Qal:	יִגְלֶה > וַיִּגְל > וַיִּגֶל akin to Second Category (b)
Niphal:	יִגָּלֶה > וַיִּגָּל no vowel shift
Piel:	יְגַלֶּה > וַיְגַל no vowel shift; the Masoretes often omitted
	dagesh forte in *yod* over a sounded *shewa*.
	See *qunmeluiy* letters in **5b**, *Note*, below.
Hiphil:	יַגְלֶה > וַיַּגְל > וַיַּגֶל as Second Category (a)
Hiphil imperative:	הַגְלֵה > הַגְל > הֶגֶל as Second Category (a)
Hithpael:	יִתְגַּלֶּה > וַיִּתְגַּל no vowel shift

Note: some apocopated forms do not go the whole way in their vowel shifts and manifest only a partial shift.

Example from בָּכָה "to weep": יִבְכֶּה > וַיֵּבְךְ, and not וַיֵּבֶךְ.

> וַיְהִי from הָיָה is the very common *waw* consecutive (apocopated) form meaning "and it came to pass"; see further, **5b** below. The form, being so important, is best committed to memory.

3de. Nouns from III-*He*/*lamed-he* roots

These nouns, Fifth Category (a), have a weak third radical *he* (which was originally *yod*); see **1fa** above. The final radical is "burnt off" or eliminated by pure long vowels יֹֽ◌–, יֹ◌– or ִי◌–. The third person suffixes are, respectively, הוּ◌– and הָ◌–; these also "burn off" or eliminate the final radical. Similarly, the first person plural suffix נוּ◌–. If it is necessary to add the new feminine ending הֹ◌–, that too "burns off" the final *he*. For example, in Isa. 7:14 הָרָה "pregnant" is a feminine adjective, where the masculine(!) would theoretically be הָרֶה. Thus, הָרֶה has the *he* of the root, while הָרָה has the *he* of the feminine ending. The second person suffixes restore the final *he* to its original *yod* (ה to י). The construct masculine singular anomalously lengthens הֹ◌– to הָ◌–.

Examples:　עָלֶה　"leaf"[5]　　　עָלִים　"leaves"
　　　　　עֲלֵה־　"leaf of"　　　עֲלֵי־　"leaves of"
　　　　　עָלִי　"my leaf"
　　　　　עָלֶיךָ　"your leaf" (singular)
　　　　　עָלֵהוּ　"his leaf"
　　　　　עָלֶהָ　"her leaf"

A number of nouns retain the original י and are preceded in the first syllable by a *shewa*.

Examples:　שְׁבִי חֲלִי חֲצִי פְּרִי גְּדִי אֲרִי

---

[5] Some forms here do not actually occur in the Hebrew Bible. In the interest of clarity, they are created according to the rules.

With suffixes added to the singular, the initial *shewa* becomes a full vowel, which may be a *patach*, *hireq* or *holem* (see Second Category nouns/adjectives). Where the first syllable has a *hateph* (directional *shewa*), the full vowel accords with the direction of the *hateph*. Where the first syllable is a simple sounded *shewa*, the full vowel is usually *hireq*.

Examples: אַרְיוֹ   "his lion"

                 פִּרְיָהּ   "her fruit"

                 חָלְיֵנוּ   "our sickness" (with *qametz-hatuph*)

                 גְּדָיִים   "kids" (approximates to First Category); cf. אֲרָיִים "lions"

3e. Hollow Verbs[6] or II-*Waw*(*Yod*)/*ayin-waw*(*yod*) Verbs

These verbs are so called because the middle radical is weak, being either a *waw* or a *yod*, the greater number being *waw*. These verbs are the *only verbs to be cited in the infinitive construct/verbal noun form*, for the reason that this form preserves the three radicals. The paradigm verb is usually קוּם "to arise".

The *Qal* perfect loses the middle radical entirely, and runs with two basic forms. From קוּם they are: ‑קָמ and ‑קַמ. The first, ‑קָמ, is used for *vowel* affformatives (endings) and also where there is *no* affformative; the second, ‑קַמ, is used with *consonantal* affformatives, thus:

קָם	קָמוּ
קָמָה	
קַמְתָּ	קַמְתֶּם ‑תֶּן
קַמְתְּ	
קַמְתִּי	קַמְנוּ

---

[6] The usual term "hollow verbs" is taken from Arabic grammars, as it describes well the obvious phenomenon of two consonants surrounding a weak middle letter. In this initial section they are set out with their full terminology; hereafter, in this Primer, they are referred to simply as "hollow verbs".

The verb בִּין "to understand" is an example of a hollow verb in *yod* (II-*Yod*). The perfect runs *exactly* as in the case of קוּם above:

בָּנוּ		בָּן
		בָּנָה
בַּנְתָּם –תֶּן		בַּנְתָּ
		בַּנְתְּ
בַּנּוּ		בַּנְתִּי

Variations in the Stative Verb ("a" type) מוּת "to die":

מֵתוּ		מֵת (a/e shift)
		מֵתָה
מַתֶּם –תֶּן		מַתָּ (from מַתְתָּ)
		מַתְּ
מַתְנוּ		מַתִּי

Stative Verb ("o" type) בּוֹשׁ "to be ashamed":

בּוֹשׁוּ		בּוֹשׁ
		בּוֹשָׁה
בָּשְׁתֶּם –תֶּן (*qametz-hatuph*)		בּשְׁתָּ
		בּשְׁתְּ
בּשְׁנוּ		בּשְׁתִּי

Qal Imperfect of קוּם:

–֞יְ –ָתּ –ָאֶ –ָנְ form the four initial preformatives. The *qametz* occurs because the syllable is open, whereas it is usually closed in other verbs. *Note*: that the *qametz* has evolved from *patach*, since the initial preformative vowel for all *Qal* imperfects is likely originally to have been "a", as it still is in Arabic.

The second syllable takes the form of the verbal noun/infinitive construct or 2ms imperative ‎קוּם–:

יָקוּם	יָקוּמוּ
תָּקוּם	תְּקוּמֶינָה
תָּקוּם	תָּקוּמוּ
תָּקוּמִי	תְּקוּמֶינָה
אָקוּם	נָקוּם

For verbs with medial *yod*, the equivalent form is ‎בִּין– as above, but with –◌ִי– in place of –וּ–.

Imperatives (derived from the imperfect): ‎קֹמְנָה   קוּמִי   קוּמוּ   קוּם

Note: The forms ‎קוּמִי/קוּם occur in the New Testament when Jesus says to the little sick girl, ‎טַלִיתָא קוּמִי "*Talitha kum(i)* – little lamb, get up" (Aramaic, Mark 5:41).

Participle: has the same form as the 3ms perfect ‎קָם and is therefore a (single syllable) First Category noun/adjective.

Hiphil Perfect: The prefix –הֶ in these verbs is lengthened to –הֵ because the syllable is open, whereas it is usually closed in other verbs.

The consonantal afformatives in these verbs are *ALL PRECEDED* by an "o" *connecting vowel*. The resulting forms resemble First Category nouns:

הֵקִים	הֵקִימוּ
הֵקִימָה	
הֲקִימֹתָ	הֲקִימֹתָם –תֶן
הֲקִימֹת	
הֲקִימֹתִי	הֲקִימֹנוּ

The imperfect preformatives, being in an open syllable, are again: –יָ –תָּ –אָ –נָ.
The second syllable is composed of the familiar –יֹ– of the *Hiphil*:

יָקִים	(3fs, 2ms)	יָקִימוּ	(3fpl, 2fpl)
תָּקִים		תָּקֵמְנָה	
תָּקִימִי		תָּקִימוּ	
אָקִים		נָקִים	

Imperatives are of the form הָקֵם. Note the shortening of the יֹ vowel to ֵ in the
2ms form. The יֹ is resumed in two of the following forms: הָקֵמְנָה הָקִימוּ הָקִימִי.

Participle: מֵקִים (ms). This is a disguised First Category noun/adjective, thus
מְקִימִים (mpl).

Niphal: This theme does not exist for קוּם, but in the interests of convenience and
clarity, the forms are listed as if they existed. The *Niphal* behaves rather as the
Hiphil, again using the "o" connecting vowel for consonantal afformatives. In the
perfect the –נ preformative of the regular verb, being now in an open syllable,
lengthens to –נָ. The medial *waw* is preserved, associated with an "o" vowel:

נָקוֹם	נָקוֹמוּ
נְקוֹמֹת	נְקוֹמֹנוּ

Imperfect:	The initial preformatives are as expected: –נָקוֹ –אֶקוֹ תָּקוֹ– יָקוֹ–
	Forms are: תְּקוֹמְנָה אֶקוֹם תְּקוֹמִי יָקוֹם
Imperatives:	הִקּוֹמְנָה הִקּוֹמוּ הִקּוֹמִי הִקּוֹם
Participle:	נָקוֹם This is a First Category noun/adjective.

3*ea*. Short forms:
These occur in the imperfect with *waw* consecutive and jussives. Any of these
forms which end with the third radical are prone to shortening:

Qal: יָקוּם > וַיָּקָם *Note*: the retracted tone, where the second ◌ָ is *qametz-hatuph*. The accent of יָקוּם is on the second syllable; the *waw* consecutive form has the accent on the –ָ–, which causes the shortening of the final syllable. This does not happen with the first person וָאָקוּם, nor, as usual, when anything follows the third radical; e.g., וַיָּקוּמוּ. The jussive is יָקֹם, shortened from יָקוּם.

Hiphil: יָקִים > וַיָּקֶם with retracted tone as above; but וַיָּקִימוּ, where the third radical is not the last letter. The jussive is יָקֵם, shortened from יָקִים.

3f. Geminate or Doubled Verbs or Double-*ayin* Verbs

This class of verbs is so named because the second and third radicals are identical. They behave in a way which is very similar to the Hollow verbs (**3d** above). Because many forms are abbreviated, the doubled radical is written only once with *dagesh forte*. Note, however, that the *dagesh*, though implicit, cannot be written when the doubled letter occurs as the final letter of a word. The usual paradigm verb is סָבַב "to go round, surround".

Qal Perfect:

סַב (סָבַב – alternative, old form)	סָבּוּ (סָבְבוּ – old form)
סַבָּה (סָבְבָה – old form)	
סַבּוֹתָ	סַבּוֹתֶם –תֶן
סַבּוֹת	
סַבּוֹתִי	סַבּוֹנוּ

Notes: 1. The connecting vowel –ו– is used for consonantal afformatives.
2. The *dagesh forte* is written when anything follows the doubled radical. It is implicit, but not written, when the doubled radical is the final letter.
3. The alternative old forms occur for 3ms, 3fs and 3pl only.

Qal Imperfect: ‏–ְי‎ ‏–ְתּ‎ ‏–ְא‎ ‏–ְנ‎ form the four initial preformatives. The *qametz* occurs because the syllable is open, whereas it is usually closed in other verbs. *Note*: the *patach* becomes *qametz*, since the initial preformative vowel for *Qal* imperfects is likely to have been "a", as it still is in Arabic. The second vowel is "o", as in the regular strong verb.

יָסֹב	יִסֹּבוּ
תָּסֹב (3fs, 2ms)	תְּסֻבֶּינָה (3fpl, 2fpl)
תָּסֹבִּי	תָּסֹבּוּ
אָסֹב	נָסֹב

Notes: 1. The connecting vowel ‏–ֶי‎ is used for the feminine plural consonantal afformatives.

2. The *dagesh forte* is written when anything follows the doubled radical. It is implicit, but not written, when the doubled radical is the final letter.

3. Again the phenomenon of the retracted tone is manifest in *waw* consecutive forms, as in Hollow verbs, above. The stress moves forward to the first syllable from the second in forms without any afformative, but excluding, as usual, the first person (see **3ea** above).

Examples:

    Qal: וַיָּסָב > יָסֹב (the second ◌ָ is a *qametz-hatuph*)

    Hiphil: וַיָּסֵב > יָסֵב

Imperatives: are, as usual, derived from the imperfect: סֹב סֹבִּי סֹבּוּ סֻבֶּינָה

Verbal Noun/Infinitive Construct: סֹב This is Fifth Category (b); see **1fb** above and **3fa** below.

Infinitive Absolute: סָבוֹב (old form).

Participle: סוֹבֵב (old form). This is a Third Category noun/adjective, as in the regular verb.

Stative Verb variant: Paradigm verb קַל (root קלל "light, unencumbered"):

Qal Perfect:	as in סבב above, but there are no alternative old forms.
Qal Imperfect:	the four preformatives are –יַ –תַ –אֶ –נַ (note a/e shift), and the second vowel is "a", as usual in all stative verbs.
	Examples: יֵקַלּוּ יֵקַל

Alternative Qal Imperfect: Geminate verbs uniquely have an alternative imperfect, sometimes called an "Aramaic imperfect". They are very simple indeed, in that the second radical combines itself with the first radical, rather than with the third (as סבב above): תִּסֹּבְנָה תִּסֹּבוּ יִסֹּב. There is no change in this form when *waw* consecutive is used, because the first radical has been strengthened by a *dagesh forte*.

Hiphil Perfect: The prefix –הִ is, in these verbs, lengthened to –הֵ because the syllable is open as in the case of the Hollow verbs. In most other verbs it is closed. The consonantal afformatives in these verbs are ALL PRECEDED by an –וֹ– connecting vowel, stressed, as in the Hollow verbs. The resulting forms resemble in their pattern First Category nouns:

הֵסַבּוּ	הֵסַב
	הֵסַבָּה
הֲסִבֹּתֶם –תֶן	הֲסִבּוֹתָ
	הֲסִבּוֹת
הֲסִבּוֹנוּ	הֲסִבּוֹתִי

Note: In the 3ms, 3fs and 3pl the second vowel is –ﹷ–, rather than the expected –יﹷ–. The phenomenon of the lengthened prefix –הֵ occurs with *vocalic* afformatives or *no* afformatives (here, third person forms).

Hiphil Imperfect: The preformatives, being in an open syllable, are again: –יַ –תַ –אַ –נַ. The second syllable has –יﹷ– rather than the familiar –יﹷ– of *Hiphils*: יָסֵב יָסֵבּוּ but תְּסִבֶּינָה

Imperatives: הֲסֵב הָסֵבִּי הָסֵבּוּ הֲסִבֶּינָה

Infinitives Construct and Absolute: הָסֵב (First Category, variant form, see participle below).

Participle: מֵסֵב מְסִבָּה This is a (disguised) First Category noun/adjective akin to גָּמָל with its plural גְּמַלִּים (see under First Category, variant form, **1ba** above).

Niphal Perfect: This behaves rather as the *Hiphil*. The –נְ preformative of the regular verb, being now in an open syllable, lengthens to –נָ. The usual *patach* precedes the doubled radical:

נָסַב	נָסַבּוּ
נָסַבָּה	
נָסַבּוֹתָ	נְסַבּוֹתֶם –תֶן
נָסַבּוֹת	
נָסַבּוֹתִי	נְסַבּוֹנוּ

Note: the usual –וֹ– connecting vowel for consonantal afformatives.

Imperfect: the initial preformatives are the regular: –נ אָס– תָּ– יִ ס–

Forms are: תִּסַבֶּינָה יִסַבּוּ אָסַב יָסַב

Participle: נָסָב נְסַבִּים This is a (disguised) First Category noun/adjective akin to גָּמָל with its plural: גְּמַלִּים (see under First Category, variant form, **1ba** above).

3fa. Nouns from geminate or doubled roots

These nouns, Fifth Category (b), see **1fb** above, are monosyllables because the second and third radicals, being identical, are usually written only once, and the *dagesh*, though implicit, cannot be written in the final letter of a word. As soon as anything is added to the monosyllable, the coalesced second and third radicals, written once, are now marked with a *dagesh forte*. There are occasionally plurals of this class which set out the two last radicals in full.

Examples: עַם "people" עַמִּי "my people" עַמֵּי־ "peoples of"

קַל "light, unencumbered" קַלִּים (pl)

תָּם "perfect" תַּמָּה "perfect" (fem)

הַר "mountain" הָרִים "mountains",[7] and sometimes הֲרָרִים (with
two letters *resh*)

שַׂר "prince" שָׂרָה "princess, Sarah"

צֵל "shadow" צִלּוֹ "his shadow" צְלָלִים "shadows". This noun also
approximates to Second Category (b) above.

חֹק "statute" חֻקִּים "statutes" חֻקֶּיךָ "your statutes". This noun also
approximates to Second Category (c) above.

A number of these nouns, with the article added, lengthen their *patach* to *qametz*.

Examples: עַם BUT הָעָם

הַר BUT הָהָר

אֶרֶץ BUT הָאָרֶץ Here, exceptionally, from Second Category (a).

3g. Guttural Verbs

There are certain general principles affecting guttural verbs which may be listed as
follows:

1. Simple sounded *shewas* beneath a guttural letter must become *hatephs*
   (directional *shewas*); e.g., *Qal* 3fs of שחט > שָׁחֲטָה; cf. the regular קָטְלָה.
   A guttural letter cannot be doubled, so that a short vowel preceding it is
   lengthened by compensation; e.g., *Piel* pf 3ms of ברך > בֵּרֵךְ (and often
   בֵּרַךְ, without a/e shift, under the influence of the guttural *resh*, see point 2,
   immediately below); cf. the regular קִטֵּל.

2. Guttural letters inhibit the a/e shift; e.g., *Piel* pf 3ms of שלח > שִׁלַּח; cf. the
   regular קִטֵּל.

---

[7] *Resh* in Masoretic Hebrew does not double, so הָרִים rather than הָרּים. It is likely that in
ancient Hebrew the *resh* doubled, as it does in Arabic.

3ga. I-Guttural/*Pe*-Guttural Verbs (Initial Guttural Verbs)

Qal Perfect: is entirely normal, except for *hateph* (directional *shewa*) –ֲ on the first radical of verbs with םֶֽתְ– ןֶֽתְ– endings: םֶֽתְּדַבֲע

Qal Imperfect in "o": the initial preformatives are –ַי –ַתּ –ַא –ַנ. This, rather than *hireq*, was the original vowel of imperfects, as in Arabic. The guttural has served to preserve the "a" vowel. The following silent *shewa* of the regular verb is replaced by an "a" *hateph* (directional *shewa*) ֲ. So, e.g., דֹמֲעַי הָנְדֹמֲעַתּ. For the 2fs, 3pl, 2mpl forms, this directional *shewa* MUST become a full *patach* to avoid the *prohibited* two sounded *shewas*: יִדְמַעַתּ וּדְמַעַי (from the *prohibited* וּדְמֲעַי)

Qal Imperfect in "a": To avoid a form composed entirely of "a" vowels, dissimilation takes place; thus the initial preformatives are –ֶי –ֶתּ –ֶא –ֶנ. The following silent *shewa* of the regular verb is replaced by a *hateph* (directional *shewa*) ֲ. So, e.g., קַזֱחֶי הָנְקַזֱחֶתּ. For the 2fs, 3pl, 2mpl, this directional *shewa* MUST become a full *seghol* to avoid the *prohibited* two sounded *shewas*: יִקְזֶחֶתּ וּקְזֶחֶי. A few verbs retain the silent *shewa* of the regular verb after the first syllable; e.g., from םַתָח, imperfect םֹתְּחֶי.

Imperatives and participles: are entirely regular.

The other themes of the verb (for these verbs – *Hiphil*, *Hophal* and *Niphal*) behave in exactly the same way as the *Qal*. Signposts only are listed here:

Niphal: (לֵטָקִי) דַמֲעַי (לַטְקִנ,) דַמֱעֶנ
Hiphil: (ליִטְקִי) דיִמֲעַי (ליִטְקִה,) דיִמֱעֶה
Hophal: (לַטְקָה) דַמֱעָה (,(לַטְקִי) דַמֲעָי, all with *qametz-hatuph*

3gb. I-*Aleph/pe-aleph* Verbs
These are a sub-class of the I-Guttural/*pe*-guttural verbs. They are few in number but very common in use: רמא "to say", הבא "to be willing", לכא "to eat", הפא "to bake", דבא "to perish".

Mnemonic: "He said, 'I am willing to eat what you bake, though I perish'".

The *Qal* perfect is quite normal. The *Qal* imperfects are in "a" and the *aleph* quiesces, taking an "o" vowel in dissimilation.[8] Thus, יֹאמַר > יַאֲמַר.

For the imperatives and the verbal noun/infinitive construct, the older initial ◌ֱ vowel is reinstated, and the second vowel, notwithstanding the imperfect in "a", is unexpectedly an "o": אֱמֹר. The infinitive construct of אמר, prefixed with *lamed*, is very common indeed, and in it the *aleph* quiesces: לֵאמֹר (from לֶאֱמֹר). The word indicates that direct speech follows, and serves as the equivalent of opening quotation marks in English. In the King James Bible it is rendered "saying…", followed by what is said. The phrase "and he said…" is one of the most common expressions in the Hebrew Bible. Its form is וַיֹּאמֶר, an a/e shift from the less common וַיֹּאמַר. (Both forms have retracted tone, see under *waw* Consecutive, **5b** below.)

3gc. II-Guttural/*Ayin*-Guttural Verbs (Medial Guttural)

Note: in what follows, the roots שחט נחם ברך have been used because ברך (not found in the *Qal*) has a medial *resh*; the other two verbs represent those with a medial guttural which is not *resh*. The following considerations apply:

1. Guttural letters in second (or third) place commonly have *Qal* imperfects and imperatives in "a". The *Piel* perfect 3ms has an "a" vowel because gutturals here inhibit the a/e shift: נִחַם יְשַׁלַּח (cf. the regular קִטֵּל יְקַטֵּל).
2. The middle radical, being a guttural letter, cannot be doubled and, consequently, the preceding "i" vowel of the *Piel* perfect lengthens to *tsere* by compensation before *resh* and *aleph*. Otherwise the "i" vowel is retained, even though the radical cannot be doubled. In the *Piel* imperfect, and the *Hithpael* perfect and imperfect, the *patach* before *resh* and *aleph* lengthens to *qametz* by compensation. In the *Pual* perfect and imperfect the short "u" vowel lengthens to *holem* by compensation.

---

[8] The reason is probably dissimilation, i.e., the avoidance of two concurrent identical vowels. The imperative and infinitive construct forms suggest that the imperfect may once have been an imperfect in "o". When the imperfect, (possibly?) under the influence of the *resh*, evolved to an "a" vowel, the "o" of the quiescent *aleph* achieved the desired dissimilation.

Perfect		Imperfect
בֵּרֵךְ	Piel	יְבָרֵךְ
בֹּרַךְ	Pual	יְבֹרַךְ
הִתְבָּרֵךְ	Hithpael	יִתְבָּרֵךְ
נִחַם	Piel	יְנַחֵם
נֻחַם	Pual	יְנֻחַם
הִתְנַחֵם	Hithpael	יִתְנַחֵם

Imperatives follow the imperfect forms, with the preformative removed. But in the case of *Niphal*, *Hiphil* and *Hithpael* forms, the preformative, as usual, is replaced by –הַ.

The *Qal* verbal noun/infinitive construct retains the "o" vowel, despite imperfect in "a": שָׁחוֹט (from שׁחט "to slaughter").

Participles: מִתְבָּרֵךְ מְבֹרָךְ מְבָרֵךְ מְנַחֵם נִשְׁחָט שׁוֹחֵט

3gd. III-Guttural/lamed Guttural Verbs (Final Guttural)
When the final letter is a guttural, it is usually preceded by an "a" vowel; thus it has an imperfect in "a". If there is a long vowel between the second and third radicals, then the "a" sound is a furtive *patach*.
   Examples:

שׁוֹלֵחַ	*Qal* active participle
שָׁלוּחַ	*Qal* passive participle
שְׁלוֹחַ	*Qal* infinitive construct
הִשְׁלִיחַ	*Hiphil* perfect 3ms
מַשְׁלִיחַ	*Hiphil* participle

All imperfects (and therefore imperatives) without afformatives have *patach* as the final vowel. In the *Piel* and *Hithpael* the a/e shift has been inhibited: (from יְשַׁלַּח) יִשְׁתַּלַּח, יְשַׁלַּח. The participles tend to retain the *tsere*: שַׁלֵּחַ. In the form יִשְׁתַּלַּח

there occurs metathesis of sibilants, i.e., the ת of the preformative –תִ֫ changes places with the first radical שׁ (see **2ef** above). This occurs because Hebrew finds it difficult to pronounce יִתְשַׁלַּח.

3ge. III-*Aleph/lamed-aleph* Verbs

The irregularities occur in this class because *aleph* has a tendency to quiesce. When *aleph* occurs at the end of a syllable, it is silent following the vowel which precedes it: (from מצא "to find") מָצָא יִמְצָא. The *patach* in both cases has lengthened to *qametz* before the quiescent *aleph*. In the *Qal* perfect the quiescent *aleph* remains throughout, except for the vocalic afformatives, where the *aleph* resumes its original function as a glottal stop: מָצְאָה מָצְאוּ. The same rule obtains in the imperfect, where vocalic afformatives occur. In stative verbs, instead of *qametz*, *tsere* is found: (from root מלא "to be full") מָלֵא מָלֵאתָ but, as expected, מָלְאוּ.

The *Niphal* forms: נִמְצָא נִמְצֵאתָ נִמְצְאוּ – the imperfect is regular.
The *Hiphil* forms: הִמְצִיא הִמְצֵאתָ הִמְצִיאוּ – the imperfect is regular.

Note: Tav afformatives do not take *dagesh lene*, because the *aleph* is quiescent.

4

The Definite Article

The definite article in Hebrew consists of *he* pointed with a *patach* and followed by *dagesh forte*, thus –◌ַה. The phenomenon may be compared to the Arabic definite article, *ʾal-* or *ʾel-* (often pronounced with a/e shift). If this article precedes certain letters in Arabic, the *l* merges with the first letter of the word which follows, e.g., *ʾal-salaam > ʾassalaam*. The article in Hebrew, then, is likely to have been originally –לַה (cf. Gen. 37:19, הַלָּזֶה for הַזֶּה), and the *dagesh forte* represents the memory of the ל, much as the acute accent in French *école* "school" represents the memory of an "s".

The guttural letters (א ה ח ע and ר) in Hebrew CANNOT be doubled or receive *dagesh forte* and, consequently, three fall-back positions are adopted when a guttural letter immediately follows the article:

1. Before א ע and ר: The *patach* lengthens to *qametz* to compensate for the lack of *dagesh forte*: הָרֹאשׁ הָעוֹף הָאָרֶח
   Certain words, usually monosyllables, change their characteristic *patach* into *qametz* under the influence of the lengthened article:
   הָאָרֶץ > אֶרֶץ, הָהָר > הַר, הָעָם > עַם, and uniquely

2. Before ה and ח: The *patach* is retained without lengthening before the guttural, which, of course, cannot be doubled or take *dagesh forte*:
   הַחֹשֶׁךְ הַהֵיכָל

3. Before הָ חָ עָ (with *qametz*): When these letters introduce the FIRST SYLLABLE OF A TWO-SYLLABLE WORD (or an unstressed syllable), the article is pointed הֶ:
   הֶעָמָל > עָמָל, הֶחָמָס > חָמָס, הֶהָרִים > הָרִים

5

The Conjunction *Waw*, *Waw* Consecutive, and Simple *Waw* with Imperfect (Jussive and Cohortative)

5a. The Conjunction *Waw*

The conjunction וְ "and" is attached directly to the beginning of nouns and adjectives (with or without the definite article). The usage is as follows:

1.   The default pointing is simple sounded *shewa*.
2.   Before the *hatephs* it is pointed with the full vowel of the direction of the *hateph*.
3.   Before sounded *shewa* and the labial letters it is pointed וּ (the labial letters are פ מ ב).

       Mnemonic: "*bump*"
4.   Before a monosyllable or a stressed syllable (especially nouns in pairs), it is pointed וָ.

Examples:
1.   וְהַיֶּלֶד "and the boy" וְאִשָּׁה "and a woman"
2.   וֶאֱמֶת "and truth" וַאֲנִי "and I"
3.   וּמִרְיָם "and Miriam" וּשְׁמוּאֵל "and Samuel"
4.   טוֹב וָרָע "good and evil"

Before *yod* with *shewa* (יְ) the *yod* collapses, producing a pure long "i" vowel: וִיהוּדָה. Similarly, but exceptionally, with *aleph*: וֵאלֹהִים > וֶאֱלֹהִים.

5b. *Waw* Consecutive

When the conjunction ו is prefixed *directly* to a verbal form (and *only* so) the result is that *waw* with an imperfect has a past meaning, while *waw* with a perfect form has a future or present meaning.[1] *Waw* added to a *perfect* form is pointed with simple sounded *shewa* and obeys the consequent rules set out in **5a** above. *Waw* added to an *imperfect* form is pointed with *patach*, and the letter following is marked with *dagesh forte*. The first person form, beginning with *aleph* (which, as a guttural, cannot be doubled), causes the vowel to lengthen from *patach* to *qametz*.

Example: וַיִּקְטֹל but וְאָקְטֹל

Note: the stress of an imperfect form is on the last syllable; but when a *waw* consecutive is prefixed to that form, the stress is upon the first syllable (now, the retracted tone).

In what follows "A" stands for perfect forms, and "B" for imperfect, imperative and participle forms. The scheme of *waw* consecutive thus runs as follows:

Past time: A + ו B + ו B + ו B, etc. "He went (A) to the city, and caught (ו B) a bus, and sat down (ו B) to lunch, and returned (ו B) to his home".

Future time: B + ו A + ו A + ו A, etc. "He will go (B) to the city, and will catch (ו A) a bus, and will sit down (ו A) to lunch, and will return (ו A) to his home".

Note: Sentences in Hebrew may start with ו A or ו B without the appearance of the initial A or B verbal form. If anything whatsoever comes between the ו and the verbal form, e.g., a negation (וְלֹא), the tense will bear its simple, straightforward form and meaning without reversal.

---

[1] This extraordinary phenomenon is not fully understood, but reasons for it can be detected by reference to the long history of the language. In Modern Hebrew pronunciation the word *waw* is pronounced "vahv"; the pronunciation "wow" remains in use in some circles.

Example: "And he went and did not eat and returned".

"And he went (וַיֵּלֶךְ = ו B) and did not eat (וְלֹא אָכַל = ו + negation A) and returned (וַיָּשָׁב = ו B)".

Two particular forms of the verb הָיָה "to become, come to pass" are an integral part of the scheme:

| וְהָיָה | "and it shall come to pass, happen" (ו A) |
| וַיְהִי | "and it happened, came to pass" (ו B) |

This latter form is derived from an apocopated imperfect, thus:

וַיְהִי > וַיְּהִי > יִהְיֶה

For היה as a III-*He*/*lamed-he* verb, see **3dd** above.

Note: The Masoretes commonly omitted *dagesh forte* over vocal/sounded *shewa* in the letters י ו ל מ נ ק (mnemonic: *qunmeluiy*).

5c. Simple *Waw* with Imperfect (Jussive and Cohortative)

It was stated above that if *waw* is prefixed *directly* onto a verbal form, the result is that *waw* plus an imperfect form has a past meaning, while *waw* plus a perfect form has a future/present meaning. There is, however, *one important exception*: *waw* pointed with a simple *shewa* (and normal consequent variations) may be added to an imperfect form (or a jussive or cohortative), which then has a *subjunctive* meaning.

Examples: "He will go to the countryside to feed the sheep" (lit., "and let him feed the sheep") = יֵלֵךְ אֶל־הַשָּׂדֶה וְיִרְעֶה אֶת־הַצֹּאן

"Come on, I want you to go to the city for me" (lit., "and let me send you to the city") = לֵךְ וְאֶשְׁלָחֲךָ אֶל־הָעִיר (or הָעִירָה)

Simple *waw* with the imperfect is a legitimate alternative to the *waw* consecutive form. The pointing indicates the difference, as does the context. By contrast, *waw* attached *directly* to a perfect form is almost always *waw* consecutive.

6

Particles, Prepositions, and Articles

6a. The Interrogative Particle

Questions are introduced by the particle –הֲ. The default pointing is –הֲ. Before simple *shewa* (to avoid the *prohibited* two sounded *shewas*) it is pointed with *patach* הַ. Before the gutturals its pointing is also הַ, but before gutturals with *qametz* it is pointed הֶ (cf. The Definite Article, **4** above). The consonant following the particle is occasionally marked with *dagesh forte*. Although the resulting appearance may be indistinguishable from the *dagesh forte* following the article, it is in fact an aid to pronunciation, rather than an indication of an erstwhile consonant (normally, but not always, לֹ), as is the case with the definite article.

6b. Inseparable Prepositions

These are: בְּ "in, with (instrument), by"; כְּ "like, as, according to"; and לְ "to, for (dative)". These are attached to the front of nouns.

Rules:
1. They are normally pointed with a simple, sounded *shewa*.
2. If a word starts with a sounded *shewa*, the usual principle must be followed, i.e., THERE CAN NEVER BE TWO SOUNDED *SHEWAS*. Consequently,
   - 2a. Before a simple, sounded *shewa* the preposition takes *hireq*: לִבְרִית בִּשְׁמוּאֵל
   - 2b. Before a *hateph* (composite, directional *shewa*) the preposition takes the full vowel of the direction of the *hateph*: לֶאֱדֹם בָּאֱדֹם

2c.   Before the stressed syllable, the preposition, now pre-tonic, is pointed with *qametz*: לָשֶׁבֶת כָּמוֹנִי

3.   When the inseparable precedes a definite noun, the *he* of the article, being weak, disappears, and the inseparable sits over the vowel of the article without the *he*:

הַכֶּלֶב "the dog"   לַכֶּלֶב "to the dog"

הָהָר "the mountain"   בָּהָר "in the mountain"

הֶעָפָר "the dust"   כֶּעָפָר "like the dust"

6ba. The Inseparables with Suffixes

כָּמוֹהוּ	לוֹ	בּוֹ
כָּמוֹהָ	לָהּ	בָּהּ
כָּמוֹךָ	לְךָ	בְּךָ
כָּמוֹךְ	לָךְ	בָּךְ
כָּמוֹנִי	לִי	בִּי
כָּהֶם –הֶן	לָהֶם –הֶן	בָּהֶם –הֶן
כָּכֶם –כֶן	לָכֶם –כֶן	בָּכֶם –כֶן
כָּמוֹנוּ	לָנוּ	בָּנוּ

Note: the –וֹמ– connecting syllable, which applies only to כְּ, but not to כְּ with the heavy suffixes: –כֶם –כֶן –הֶם –הֶן

6c. מִן Min

The preposition מִן "from" is both a separated and an inseparable preposition. It is more commonly a *separated* preposition when it precedes nouns with the *article*. It is ALWAYS an *inseparable* preposition with *indefinite nouns*. When it is inseparable, the *nun* merges with the first letter of the following word, which then carries *dagesh forte* in memory of the *nun*. If the first letter is a guttural, which cannot take *dagesh forte*, the *hireq* is lengthened to *tsere* by compensation.

Definites: מִן־הַלֵּב "from the heart"   מִן־הָהָר "from the mountain"
Indefinites: מִמִּצְרַיִם "from Egypt"   מֵאֶרֶץ "from a land"

6ca. *Min* with Suffixes

Since there is very considerable gemination (doubling) of the letters, there is no alternative but to commit the forms to memory:

מִמֶּנּוּ (for מִנְנָהוּ) "from him"   מֵהֶם מֵהֶן– "from them" (m/f pl)
מִמֶּנָּה "from her"
מִמְּךָ "from you" (ms)   מִכֶּם מִכֶּן– "from you" (m/f pl)
מִמֵּךְ "from you" (fs)
מִמֶּנִּי "from me"   מִמֶּנּוּ "from us" (same form as "from him")

6d. אֶת־ (object) and אֶת־ ("with")

6d*a.* אֶת־ when it signifies the definite object is always used with the article, with names of places and persons, and with nouns made definite by a suffix. It is also used before a construct and its definite absolute. It is NOT used with indefinite objects. It simply precedes the definite noun with a *maqqeph* (essentially a hyphen).

With suffixes אֶת־ "O b j E c t" (*sic* a memory aid) takes an "O" vowel, and with heavy suffixes an "E" vowel, thus (the forms below may also be written with י, e.g., אוֹתִי):

אֹתוֹ   אֹתָם אֶתְ–ֶן
אֹתָהּ
אֹתְךָ   אֶתְכֶם כֶן–
אֹתָךְ
אֹתִי   אֹתָנוּ

6d*b*. אֶת־ meaning "with" is homonymous and appears in exactly the same way.

> With suffixes אֶת־ "w **I T** h" (also a memory aid) takes *hireq* throughout, and
> the ת doubles throughout, thus:
>
> אִתּוֹ   אִתָּם −ם
>
> אִתָּהּ
>
> אִתָּךְ   אִתְּכֶם −כֶן
>
> אִתָּךְ
>
> אִתִּי   אִתָּנוּ

Vocabulary

Aleph

אֶבֶן "stone". Second Category (a) noun; cf. Ebenezer "stone of help".

אָדָם "Man (*homo*)", i.e., "human" in a generic sense. First Category noun, but in view of its meaning, there are no inflections. Proper name "Adam".

אֲדָמָה "ground, earth, dirt". First Category feminine noun. Connected with אָדָם; "God formed אָדָם from the אֲדָמָה …" (Gen. 2:7).

אַדֶּרֶת "cloak, mantle". Second Category (a) feminine noun, **1cc**. The first syllable is unalterable.

אָהֵב "he loved". Stative verb in "e". אַהֲבָה "love". Sixth Category feminine noun.

אֹהֶל "tent". Second Category (c) noun.

אוֹר "light". Fourth Category noun. Cf. feminine Jewish proper names: אוֹרָה, אוֹר-לִי.

אֹזֶן "ear". Second Category (c) noun. אָזְנַיִם (*qametz-hatuph*) "two ears".

אָח "brother". Irregular First Category noun. Cf. Ahijah "my brother is Yah(weh)".

אַחֲרֵי "after". Sixth Category.

אִישׁ "man". Irregular. Cf. the regular אֲנָשִׁים "men"; אִשָּׁה "woman" (original אִנְשָׁה); thus, אִשׁ < אִנְשׁ > אִישׁ, because *dagesh forte* is not written in a final letter, an inserted *yod* compensates. The construct of אִשָּׁה is irregular, though, as usual, it uses the old feminine ending. It takes the form אֵשֶׁת; cf. the famous אֵשֶׁת-חַיִל of Prov. 31:10 (lit.) "woman of strength". It is to *this* form, Second Category Noun (b), **1c** above, that the suffixes are attached: e.g., אִשְׁתִּי "my wife", אִשְׁתְּךָ "your (2ms) wife". אֲנָשִׁים is a First Category plural noun.

אָכַל "he ate". Cf. I-*Aleph/pe-aleph* verb. Imperfect is יֹאכַל; cf. אָמַר below. אָכְלָה, אֹכֶל "food". Second Category (c) nouns.

אֶל- and עַל- "to" (motion towards and of speech "to") and "upon, over, above", respectively. Proper name "El Al", the name of the Israeli airline, and Hos. 11:7. First Category plural forms, see explanation in **1bd** above. Some nine common nouns may alternatively express "motion towards" by adding as a suffix *qametz-he* of direction (◌ָה−).

      Examples: הָעִיר > הָעִירָה "to the city" מִצְרַיִם > מִצְרַיְמָה "to Egypt (lit., Egypt-ward)"

אֵלֶּה "these" (masc and fem).

אֱלֹהִים "god, gods, God". The plural form is a so-called plural of majesty when indicating God (the only God). Sixth Category noun. The singular אֱלוֹהַּ is attested but rare in Hebrew; a comparable form is known in Aramaic; cf. Mark 15:34, אֱלֹהִי *Eloi* "my God".

אָמֵן "firm, reliable". First Category adjective. "Amen" is used liturgically as a response in prayer, indicating agreement. Cf. Jesus' words, "Amen, Amen (Verily, verily), I say unto you…" (e.g., John 10:1).

69

אָמַר "he said". I-*Aleph/pe-aleph* verb, see explanation in **3g*b***. Imperfect יֹאמַר and, with *waw* consecutive, וַיֹּאמֶר (a/e shift); cf. אָכַל above. These verbs have a collapsed *aleph* "o" vowel in the imperfect. The Arabic cognate has the meaning "order, command"; cf. ʾemir "commander, Emir". Also ʾemir al-baHr "commander of the sea" > "admiral" in English. There are times when the Hebrew אָמַר comes close to the Arabic meaning, e.g., Gen. 1:3ff., "…and God said (commanded)…".

אֱמֶת (from אֲמֶנֶת) "reliability, truth"; Second Category (b) feminine noun; note *shewa* in the first syllable. With suffix אֲמִתּוֹ, where dagesh marks the original *nun*.

אֲנַחְנוּ "we".

אֲנִי "I".

אָסַף "he collected".

אֲרִי "lion". Fifth Category (a) noun.

אֶרֶץ "land, earth". Second Category (a) feminine noun. Note the unique irregularity that, with the article, the original "a" vowel, lengthened, replaces the normal *seghol*; so הָאָרֶץ, NOT הָאֶרֶץ. In modern Hebrew הארץ denotes the Land (of Israel) and is also the name of a national newspaper.

אָרַר "he cursed". Geminate/Double-*ayin* verb.

אֲשֶׁר "who, which", etc. (or, with apologies, in English slang "wot"). Sixth Category, no changes ever made to this.

Beth

בדל, הִבְדִּיל "he separated, distinguished". The verb is normally used in the *Hiphil*.
הַבְדָּלָה The *havdalah* prayers, which render thanks for the distinctions of life, e.g., day and night (Rabbinic Judaism).

בָּזַז "he plundered". Geminate/double-*ayin* verb; cf. Isaiah's son מַהֵר שָׁלָל חָשׁ בַּז; Isa. 8:1-4.

בּוֹא "to come"; בָּא "he came"; הֵבִיא *Hiphil* "he brought".

בָּחַר "he chose".

בֵּין "between". Fourth Category, and unchangeable. The plural form בֵּינוֹת is also used and is, again, unchangeable. The root is בִּין "to understand", because understanding consists of discriminating between things.

בַּיִת "house". Fourth Category noun; cf. Beth-el, Beth-lehem. The plural בָּתִּים (Sixth Category) is very irregular and contains a long vowel in a closed unaccented syllable.

בָּכָה "he wept". III-*He/lamed-he* verb.

בֵּן "son". Irregular, akin to Second Category (b), monosyllable. With suffixes the first syllable drops to *shewa*: בְּנִי "my son", בְּנֵךְ "thy (2fs) son". With 2ms and 2pl suffixes, to avoid the forbidden two sounded *shewas*: בִּנְךָ, בִּנְכֶם "thy/your son" (cf. שֵׁם below). The plural בָּנִים "sons" is a straightforward First Category form.

בָּנָה "he built". III-*He/lamed-he* verb.

בִּקְעָה "valley". Second Category (b) feminine noun; cf. *Bekaa* in Lebanon.

בֹּקֶר "morning". Second Category (c) noun. בֹּקֶר טוֹב (Modern Hebrew) "Good morning".

בִּקֵּשׁ "he sought" *Piel*. Cf. בְּבַקָּשָׁה (Modern Hebrew) "please, at your service", a usage similar to German *Bitte*, also as a response to "thank-you"; cf. Spanish *de nada*.

בָּרָא "he created". III-*Aleph/lamed-aleph* verb; only predicated of God.

בָּרִיא "healthy". First Category. (Modern Hebrew) לַבְּרִיוּת "good health, to your health" = a wish after a sneeze, etc., the English/American equivalent of "bless you!".

בֵּרַךְ "he blessed" *Piel*; בְּרָכָה "blessing". First Category feminine noun. בָּרוּךְ "blessed, fortunate" *Qal* passive ptc. First Category. Cf. Baruch, Jeremiah's secretary; Arabic names *Mubarrak* and *Barak*.

בַּת "daughter" (Arabic *bint*); disguised Second Category (b) monosyllable. בִּתִּי "my daughter". The *dagesh* in the *taw* represents the memory of the *nun* < בִּנְתִי "my daughter" as in Arabic. בָּנוֹת "daughters" (pl). First Category.

בְּתוֹךְ "in, within". This is a combination of preposition בְּ and תוֹךְ– (cstr); see תָּוֶךְ below.

Gimel

גִּבּוֹר "valiant (man), mighty warrior". Cf. proper name Gabriel (Arabic, Jibreel).

גָּדוֹל "big, great". First Category adjective (noun). The name (Mary) Magdalene refers to the fortress town by the Sea of Galilee from which she came. Migdal, or Magdal in Palestinian Jewish tradition, is then a place name, meaning "big construction, tower, fortress". גֹּדֶל "greatness". Second Category (c) noun.

גְּדִי "kid". Fifth Category (a) noun. Cf. Ein Gedi ("spring of the goat-kid") near the Dead Sea, where ibexes are still plentiful.

גִּיל "to rejoice"; also, *per contra*, "to tremble". Hollow verb with יִ rather than ו.

גָּלָה "he revealed, uncovered"; also "went into exile". III-*He/lamed-he* verb.

גָּלַל "he rolled". Geminate/doubled verb; cf. (Aramaic) גָּלְגָּלְתָּא *Golgotha*, (Hebrew) גֻּלְגֹּלֶת *Gulgolet* "a skull" as "round" (John 19:17). Also גַּל "wave, roller" (Ps. 42:8). Fifth Category (b) noun.

גָּנַב "he stole". גַּנָּב "thief". Note the the vowel arrangment in קַטָּל "killer, assassin", the *qattāl* pattern for nouns denoting occupation; cf. טַבָּח below.

גֹּרֶן "threshing floor". Second Category (c) noun.

Daleth

דִּבֶּר "he spoke". The *Piel* of the root דבר. The 3ms perfect has a *seghol* in place of the regular (*Piel*) *tsere*. The verb is normally used in the *Piel*.

דָּג "fish". First Category, monosyllable.

דָּם "blood". Cf. Acts 1:19 *Acel-dama* "field of blood"; דָּמִים "bloodguiltiness" (abstract plural). First Category, monosyllable.

דֶּרֶךְ "way, path". Second Category (a). From דָּרַךְ "he trod"; thus > "a trodden path".

דָּרַשׁ "he sought". Cf. *Midrash*, as matters "sought out".

He

הִגִּיד "he told, reported". *Hiphil* of root נגד (*Qal* not used).

הוּא "he"; הִיא "she"; מִי "who?". These three are unalterable forms.

> Mnemonic: מִי is "who", and הוּא is "he", and הִיא is "she".
>
> Or… "If who is he, and he is she, who is me?"

הָיָה "to become, happen, come to pass, turn out". It can sometimes be rendered by the English verb "to be", but it is always safer to try "become" etc., first. III-*He/lamed-he* verb.

הֵיכָל "palace, temple". First Category with pure long, unalterable first syllable.

הָלַךְ "he walked, went". I-*Yod/pe-yod* verb, one of the Common Six. Initial *he* represents a *yod*. This is the only I-*Yod/pe-yod* verb which has *he* in the *Qal* perfect. The Talmudic concept *Halakah* is derived from this verb and denotes how to walk (through life), hence, ethics; cf. Ps. 119, *passim*.

הִלֵּל "he praised" (*Piel*; *Qal* not in use). Imperative as in הַלְלוּ־יָהּ "Praise the Lord!"; cf. תְּהִלָּה below (for the absence of *dagesh* in the first *lamed* of הַלְלוּ, see **5b** above).

הֵקִים "he raised, established"; *Hiphil* of קוּם "to arise".

הָרָה "he(!) conceived, became pregnant". III-*He/lamed-he* verb. The form הָרָה in Isa. 7:14 is a feminine adjective with the meaning "pregnant".

הִתְפַּלֵּל "he prayed" (lit. "he interposed himself"); *Hithpael* of פלל (*Qal* not used). See תְּפִלָּה below.

Waw (No entries)

Zayin

זֶבַח "sacrifice". Second Category (b) noun. The final ח has prevented the a/e shift in the second syllable; cf. זֶרַע below. מִזְבֵּחַ "altar" as "place of sacrifice". Third Category noun.

זָהָב "gold". First Category noun.

זָכַר "he remembered"; cf. Zechariah "God (Yah) has remembered" or "Let God (Yah) remember".

זָקֵן "old". First Category adjective (strictly a stative participle, and also used as a noun, "old man, elder").

זֶרַע "seed, children". Second Category (b) noun; cf. יִזְרְעֶ־אֵל Jezreel (valley), "God sows".

Heth

חָבָא "he hid". *Hithpael* הִתְחַבֵּא "he hid himself".

חָדָשׁ "new". First Category adjective. חֹדֶשׁ "month, moon, new moon", as "renewing". Second Category (c) noun.

חָזָק "strong". First Category adjective.

חָיָה "he lived". III-*He*/*lamed-he* verb.

    חַי "living"; חַיִּים "life". The latter form is an abstract plural; cf. רַחֲמִים below.

    חַיָּה "animal", as something "living". Sixth Category feminine noun.

חָטָא "he sinned". III-*Aleph*/*lamed-aleph* verb.

חָכָם "wise". First Category noun/adjective. חָכְמָה "wisdom". Second Category (c) feminine noun.

חֳלִי "sickness". Fifth Category (a), akin to Second Category (c) noun, e.g., חָלְיוֹ "his sickness".

    חֹלֶה "sick, ill person". III-*He*/*lamed-he* participle. Cf. Modern Hebrew בֵּית־חֹלִים "hospital".

חָמַם "he was hot, became warm". Geminate/doubled verb.

חָנַן "he was gracious, showed favour". Geminate/doubled verb; cf. Hannan, Hannah, Anna, Ann(e).

    חֵן "grace, favour". Second Category (b) noun, monosyllable; also Fifth Category (b) noun. Cf. Phoenician Hannibal, "grace of *Ba'al*".

חֶסֶד "lovingkindness". Second Category (a) noun.

    חָסִיד "faithful, devout". First Category; cf. חֲסִידִים "pious persons".

חֶרֶב "sword". Second Category (a) noun.

חֹשֶׁךְ "darkness, (the) dark". Second Category (c) noun.

חָתַם "he sealed" (a document). I-Guttural/*pe*-guttural verb.

Teth

טַבָּח "cook, guardsman" (Gen. 37:36); cf. גַּנָּב above, for *qattāl* form denoting occupation. Sixth Category noun.

טָהוֹר "pure, (ritually) clean". First Category adjective.

טוֹב "good, useful". Sixth Category adjective.

טָמֵא "impure, (ritually) unclean". First Category adjective.

Yod

יָד "hand". First Category, feminine, monosyllable; dual יָדַיִם "(two) hands".

יָדַע "he knew". I-*Yod*/*pe-yod* verb, one of the Common Six; see **3b** above. The word is stative, but by reason of the guttural third letter, the second vowel of the 3ms does not follow the common stative a/e shift.

יוֹם "day". Fourth Category; irregular plural יָמִים is First Category. יוֹם־כִּפּוּר *Yom Kippur*, Day of Atonement. The word should be distinguished from יָם "sea", because the forms are very similar.

    Mnemonic: יוֹם > יָמִים "days"; יָם > יַמִּים "seas".

יָכֹל "he was able". I-*Yod*/*pe-yod* stative verb in "o"; see further, **2f** above.

יָלַד "he bore"(!). I-*Yod*(*waw*)/*pe-yod*(*waw*) verb. The original initial *waw* reappears in the *Niphal* and *Hiphil* of this verb; see I-*Yod*(*waw*)/*pe-yod*(*waw*) verbs and the Common Six, **3b** above. Cf. Arabic *walad* "boy".

    יֶלֶד "boy". Second Category (a) noun; יַלְדָּה "girl".

יָם "sea, lake". First Category monosyllable. Irregular plural is Fifth Category (b). For mnemonic, see יוֹם, above. N.B. יַם־כִּנֶּרֶת Sea of Galilee, (lit.) "Harp-Sea"; יַם־הַמֶּלַח Dead Sea, (lit.) "Salt-Sea"; יַם־סוּף (lit.) "Reed Sea", "Red Sea" from the Greek translation.

יָסַף "he added". Cf. יוֹסֵף "Joseph", "God adds", i.e., lots of descendants.

יֳפִי "beauty". Akin to Second Category (c) with original י as third radical (rather than ה); e.g., יָפְיָהּ "her beauty"; cf. Joppa (Arabic *Jaffa*; Modern Hebrew יָפוֹ).

יָפֶה "fair, beautiful". Fourth Category adjective from III-*He*/*lamed-he* root.

יָצָא "he went out". I-*Yod*/*pe-yod* verb with III-*Aleph*/*lamed-aleph* ending, one of the Common Six, see **3b** above. Cf. Modern Hebrew יְצִיאָה "exit".

יָקָר "precious, dear". First Category adjective.

יָרֵא "he was fearful, he feared". III-*Aleph*/*lamed-aleph*, also I-*Yod*/*pe-yod*, keeping its *yod* in *Qal* imperfect.

יָרַד "he went down, descended". I-*Yod*/*pe-yod*, and one of the Common Six, see **3b** above. יַרְדֵּן "the Jordan" (as "going down"). Modern Hebrew יֹרֵד "go-er down", i.e., an "emigrant" from Israel; cf. עלה below.

יָרָה "he threw, shot" *Qal*; "he showed, he taught" *Hiphil*. III-*He*/*lamed-he* verb; cf. תּוֹרָה below.

יָרַשׁ "he inherited, he took possession". I-*Yod*/*pe-yod* verb. The *Qal* imperfect behaves as a pure *yod* verb, and retains the *yod* of the root; the *Hiphil* perfect and imperfect employ *waw* like the Common Six, cf. **3c** above.

יָשַׁב "he sat, dwelt, inhabited". I-*Yod*/*pe-yod* and one of the Common Six, see **3b** above. Cf. יְשִׁיבָה *Yeshiva* "Torah academy", and מוֹשָׁב "settlement, dwelling place".

יָשַׁע "he saved". *Hiphil* only; I-*Yod*(waw)/*pe-yod*(waw) verb. Cf. *hosanna* from הוֹשִׁיעָה־נָּא. The name "Jesus" יֵשׁוּעַ is a contracted form of this root (Matt. 1:21).

Kaph

כַּאֲשֶׁר "when, as".

כָּבֵד "he was heavy", so "honourable", and also "obtuse"; as a noun "liver". All these concepts derive from the basic meaning of "heaviness". Stative verb in "e"; the 3ms perfect and participle/adjective take the same form. First Category adjective.

כֹּהֵן "priest". Third Category.

כּוֹכָב "star". First Category, with unchangeable first syllable (because it is a pure long vowel). כּוֹכָבִים (pl). Bar Kokhba (Aramaic), second-century Jewish revolutionary leader.

כּוּן "to be firm". Hollow verb (II-*Waw*). *Hiphil* הֵכִין "he made firm, set up, established, prepared". Cf. Modern Hebrew כֵּן "yes" (lit. "right!, correct!").

כִּי "that, because, when". Unalterable form.

כֹּל "all"; strictly, a noun meaning "totality". The word functions as a collective; "all the king's horses" in Hebrew is expressed by "totality (of) the king's horses". The word is a Fifth Category (b) noun, and the root is כלל; the most common form is the construct כָּל־ (qametz-hatuph). With suffixes the form is ־כָּל, e.g., "all of us" is כֻּלָּנוּ. (The short "u" vowel and the short "o" vowel are closely related in Hebrew.)

כְּמוֹ "like, as, such as".

כָּסָה "he covered, obliterated". III-He/lamed-he verb, Piel only.

כֶּסֶף "silver, money". Second Category (a) noun.

כֹּפֶר "ransom". Second Category (c) noun; cf. יוֹם־כִּפּוּר "Yom Kippur" Day of Atonement.

כֶּרֶם "vineyard". Second Category (a); cf. כַּרְמֶל "(Mt.) Carmel".

כָּרַת "he cut". Note: "he made a covenant" is expressed by כָּרַת בְּרִית "he cut a covenant".

כָּתַב "he wrote"; כְּתוּבִים "the Writings" as part of the Hebrew Bible. Arabic kitaab "book".

Lamed

לְ "to, for, (with) reference (to)". This is equivalent to the Dative, and in earlier Hebrew is not used for motion or speech "to" (someone), where ־אֶל was used.

לֹא "no, not".

לָבָן "white"; cf. Laban in Genesis. First Category noun.

לַיְלָה "night" (Arabic layl^un and fem proper name: Laylah, Leila). The הָ is *not* the mark of the feminine, but a rare survival of the old accusative ending; cf. Modern Greek, καλη νυκτα "good night". Fourth Category. The construct is לֵיל־, the plural is לֵילוֹת; in view of its meaning, there are otherwise no inflections.

לָמַד "he learned"; Piel causative לִמֵּד "he taught"; cf. *Talmud*.

לָמָּה "why?" (lit. "for what?"). Cf. (Aramaic) lama sabachthani "why hast Thou forsaken me?" (Mark 15:34).

לָקַח "he took". See verbs of "Giving" and "Taking", section **3aɑ** above.

Mem

מְאֹד "very, (lit.) muchness". Sixth Category noun.

מָדַד "he measured". Geminate/doubled verb; cf. Modern Hebrew מַדְחֹם "thermometer" (מַד + חֹם = "measure" + "heat").

מַה מָה מֶה, forms of מַה "what?" The various forms are deployed exactly as the definite article; see **4** above.

מוּת "to die". Hollow (II-*Waw*) stative verb. 3ms perfect is מֵת (a/e shift from מַת). Note: (the game of chess) "checkmate", "the king is dead" (Persian/Arabic).

מָחָה "he destroyed". III-*He/lamed-he* verb.

מִי "who?"; see הוּא above.

מַיִם "water". Fourth Category noun (pl). The letter מ *mem*. The letter originates with a wavy drawing for "water". Apparently a dual form, but in fact the *yod* is a root letter. The *yod* of the plural is not written.

מֵינֶקֶת "nurse, wetnurse". Second Category (b) feminine noun from root יָנַק "to suck". The first syllable is unalterable.

מָלֵא "he was full". Stative verb in "e"; III-*Aleph/lamed-aleph* verb. Causative *Piel* is מִלֵּא "he filled", as in "he caused (it) to be full".

מַלְאָךְ "messenger, angel". First Category. The root is לאך; cf. and contrast מֶלֶךְ "king". Cf. מַלְאָכִי Malachi "my messenger".

מִלְחָמָה "war". Construct מִלְחֶמֶת, which generates suffixed forms. Second Category (a) feminine noun; see **1cc** above.

מֶלַח "salt"; the noun מַלָּח means "a sailor". See Nouns of Occupation, *Piel* **2eb** above, and compare colloquial English "salt" and American "salty dog", each denoting "a sailor"; cf. **1cb** n. 4.

מֶלֶךְ "king"; מַלְכָּה "queen" and Arabic *malik* indicate that the word has a/e shifted. Second Category (a). Compound proper names: Melchizedek, Abimelech.

מַמְלָכָה "kingdom". The construct is מַמְלֶכֶת, which generates forms for suffixes, and is a Second Category (a) feminine noun, **1cc** above. The first syllable is unalterable.

מִן "from". There is very considerable gemination or doubling of letters when suffixes are attached; see **6ca** above.

מָנָה "he counted". III-*He/lamed-he* verb. Cf. (Aramaic) Belshazzar's *mene mene tekel upharsin* "God has counted, numbered the days of your kingdom" (Dan. 5:25).

מָצָא "he found". Cf. מָצָא אִשָּׁה מָצָא טוֹב "he (who) has found a wife, has found (something) good" (Prov. 18:22).

מִצְוָה "command, commandment"; cf. Jewish *Bar-/Bat-Mitzvah* "son/daughter of the commandment".

מִצְרַיִם "Egypt" (dual, reflecting Upper and Lower Egypt, though this point is debated); cf. Arabic *misr* "Egypt".

מָקוֹם "place, establishment". First Category noun. See root קוּם below.

מָרַר "he was bitter". Geminate/doubled verb, stative verb.

מַר "bitter"; מָרָה (fs); cf. Ruth 1:20, Naomi and Mara. (The word as a noun means "bitterness".) See under שַׂר "prince, official". *Note*: this class of monosyllabic nouns have a short, closed syllable in the masculine, but as soon as an ending is affixed the vowel under the first letter lengthens to ָ, since it has become an open syllable. The words are Fifth Category (b), see **3fa** above, though in Masoretic Hebrew the ר is not doubled, as once it was.

מֹשֶׁה "Moses". Egyptian word meaning "child, son" without the theophoric element; cf. Egyptian Tutmose (with the theophoric element Tut), the name of a Pharaoh.

מָשָׁל "proverb, simile". First Category. Basic meaning, "comparison"; cf. the canonical book מִשְׁלֵי "the Proverbs of (Solomon)".

מָשַׁל "to rule". This is a homonym and has no connections with the previous entry.
Mnemonic: "The Ma(r)shal rules the West".

מִשְׁפָּט "justice, judgment, custom". First Category noun. See root שָׁפַט below.

Nun

נָבִיא "prophet". First Category noun. The collocation of vowels (◌ִי \ ◌ָ) often denotes a status or appointment; cf. פָּקִיד "officer", below. The Jewish name for the Hebrew Bible is תּוֹרָה נְבִיאִים וּכְתוּבִים, of which the acronym is תַּנַךְ *Tanak.*

נגד *Hiphil* only, הִגִּיד "he made clear, he told, he recounted". I-*Nun/pe-nun* verb.

נֶדֶר "vow". Second Category (b) noun; cf. the liturgical כָּל-נִדְרֵי of the Day of Atonement; also of Nazirites as "takers of a vow" (Num. 6:2, 21).

נָטָה "he stretched". III-*He/lamed-he* verb, also I-*Nun/pe-nun* verb. Noun מִטָּה "bed" (as a place of "stretching").

נָכָה "he smote, hit, struck". III-*He/lamed-he* verb, *Hiphil* only; e.g., יַכֶּה הִכָּה and (retracted tone) וַיַּךְ; see **3dd** above.

נָסָה "he tested"; *Piel* only, *Qal* not used. See further מַסָּה *Massah,* the place of testing in the wilderness (contracted from מַנְסָה) (Ps. 95:8).

נָפַל "he fell". I-*Nun/pe-nun* verb. Noun מַפֶּלֶת "carcass, ruin", i.e., as "fallen".

נֶפֶשׁ "throat, self, soul, person". Second Category (a) noun.

נָשָׂא "he lifted, carried (up)". I-*Nun/pe-nun*, also III-*Aleph/lamed-aleph* verb.
Mnemonic: "NASA has lift-off".

נָתַן "he gave, placed, set". I-*Nun/pe-nun* verb; cf. Nathan the prophet (without theophoric element), יְהוֹנָתָן Jonathan.

Samek

סָבַב "he turned, turned around, surrounded". Geminate/doubled verb.
סָבִיב "around". First Category noun, used adverbially.

סוּס "horse". Sixth Category unchangeable.

סוּר "to turn aside"; *Hiphil* "to remove". Hollow verb (II-*Waw*).

סֵפֶר "scroll, book". Second Category (b) noun. סוֹפֵר "scribe". Third Category. The feminine form סוֹפֶרֶת (see **1da** and **2c** above), is the so-called Feminine of Office, and denotes a masculine "scribe"; cf. קוֹהֶלֶת below. In Modern Hebrew the word means a "female author".

Ayin

עֶבֶד "servant". Second Category (a). עֶבֶד־מֶלֶךְ "servant of the king" (designation of the Ethiopian servant in Jer. 38:7); also Obadiah "servant of Yah(weh)"; cf. Arabic *Abdullah* "servant of Allah".

עֲבוֹדָה "service, work, worship". Cf. Talmud Tractate *Abodah Zarah* "foreign worship, idolatry".

עָבַר "he passed, crossed (over)". Cf. עִבְרִי "a Hebrew (man)"; עִבְרִית "a Hebrew woman" or "Hebrew language". Modern Hebrew exhortation: עִבְרִי לְמֹד עִבְרִית "If you are Jewish, learn Hebrew."

עַד "up to, until".

עוֹד "yet, still". The word is strictly a Sixth Category noun, meaning "continuance", used adverbially.

עוֹלָם "age, the universe, world". First Category noun, with a huge range of meanings: עַד־עוֹלָם "to eternity, forever"; מֵעוֹלָם "from of old"; מֶלֶךְ־הָעוֹלָם "king of the universe" (used to address God in Jewish prayer); הָעוֹלָם הַזֶּה "this age"; הָעוֹלָם הַבָּא "the age to come".

עַיִן "eye" or "spring". Fourth Category noun; dual עֵינַיִם "(two) eyes".

עִיר "city" (fs noun, as are many cities and countries). Sixth Category; plural irregular: עָרִים is Sixth Category, because the *qametz* is never reduced, so construct plural and heavy suffixes plural are עָרֵי and עָרֵיכֶם –הֶם, rather than the (First Category) expected עֲרֵיכֶם.

עָלָה "he ascended, went up". III-*He/lamed-he* verb. Modern Hebrew עֹלֶה "a go-er up", i.e., an "immigrant" to Israel; also עֲלִיָּה "going up", i.e., "immigration"; cf. ירד above.

עַל "upon, over, on top". Standing on its own there are no changes; for עַל with suffixes, see First Category **1bd** above. (Modern Israel) El Al, the name of the national airline, meaning "to, on top". The phrase occurs originally in the prophet Hosea with the sense "(you do not look) upwards", meaning "to God" (Hos. 11:7).

עָמַד "he stood". Cf. עֲמִידָה, the standing or central prayer of Jewish Synagogue worship, because it is recited while standing.

עָמוֹק "deep". First Category adjective. עֲמֻקִּים (pl); see **1ba** above. Cf. Modern Hebrew notice in swimming pools מַיִם עֲמֻקִּים "deep water".

עָנָה There are four homonymous roots ענה: I. "he answered"; II. "he occupied himself, was busy with"; III. "he was oppressed, afflicted"; IV. "he sang". All are III-*He/lamed-he* verbs, also I-Guttural.

עֳנִי "affliction". Fifth Category (a) noun, akin to Second Category (c) retaining its original י as the third radical, see **3de** above; e.g. עָנִיוֹ, from root III. in the preceding entry.

עָפָר "dust". First Category with initial guttural.

עֵץ "tree" or "trees" (collectively); עֵצִים (pl). Sixth Category nouns; note construct (pl) עֲצֵי־.

עֶרֶב "evening". Second Category (a) noun. Modern Hebrew עֶרֶב טוֹב "Good evening".

עָרוֹם "naked". First Category, variant form, see **1b*a*** above; עֲרֻמִּים "nakednesses" (pl).

עָשָׂה "he did, made". I-Guttural/*pe*-guttural, III-*He/lamed-he* verb; מַעֲשֶׂה "work", Fifth Category.

עַתָּה "now".

Peh

פֶּה "mouth". Construct and before suffixes פִּי. Fifth Category (a) noun (III-*He/lamed- he*), where the final ה was originally י.

פָּנִים "face" (the concept is plural in Hebrew). First Category. The word is extremely important in that, combined with the preposition ל, it denotes "before" (in the sense of space and time). The construct of פָּנִים is פְּנֵי and, combined with ל, produces לִפְנֵי־ "before (the face of)"; thus, לִפְנֵי־הַמֶּלֶךְ "before (the face of) the king". The construct form is used before the heavy suffixes, כֶם — כֶן — הֶם — הֶן —; e.g., לִפְנֵיהֶם. The other suffixes, being First Category, follow the collocation of vowels as in דְּבָרִים : לְפָנַי, לְפָנֶיךָ, etc. It is an *extremely common mistake* to use the construct form לִפְנֵי before forms other than those with heavy suffixes.

לְפָנִים "formerly, of old". Cf. לְאָחוֹר "hereafter, the future", suggesting a rower's 'view' of history, i.e., the past is before you and the future behind.

פָּקַד "he made arrangements (for), he appointed".

פָּקִיד "an officer" (as "one appointed"). The form denotes status or appointment; cf. נָבִיא "prophet" with the same collocation of vowels (◌ִי \ ◌ָ) above.

פַּר "young bull", פָּרָה "cow"; see further the parallel שַׂר "prince".

פְּרִי "fruit". Fifth Category (a) noun; cf. פְּרִי־הַבֶּטֶן "fruit of the womb" (Luke 1:42, a Hebrew calque).

Tsade

צָבָא "army, warfare, host". First Category noun. צְבָאוֹת (pl) "hosts, armies". In Christian liturgy "Lord God of *sabaoth*"; "YHWH of Hosts" (Isa. 6:3).

צֶדֶק "correctness". Second Category (b). Melchizedek, meaning "my king is צֶדֶק", with צֶדֶק as possibly the name of a Canaanite god.

צְדָקָה First Category feminine noun with the same meaning.

צַדִּיק "a just man" (as "correct"). Sixth Category; cf. אַבְנֵי־צֶדֶק "stones of correctness", i.e., "standard weights".

צִוָּה "he commanded". *Piel* only; III-*He/lamed-he* verb. Cf. Jewish *Bar-/Bat-Mitzvah* "son/daughter of the commandment".

צֵל "shadow". Fifth Category (b) noun; cf. צֵל־מָוֶת "shadow of death" (Ps. 23:4).

צֶלֶם "image". Cf. Modern Hebrew צַלָּם "photographer"; compare גַּנָּב "thief" and the form קַטָּל denoting occupation, see **2e*b*** above.

צַר "enemy, adversary"; צָרָה, צָרִים (fs and mpl); cf. further שַׂר "prince".

Qoph

קָדוֹשׁ "holy". First Category adjective; cf. *Qaddish* and *Qiddush*, respectively, the Jewish Prayer for the Dead, and Sanctification of the Cup. Arabic *ʾal-quds* "the holy place", i.e., Jerusalem.

קָהָל "congregation, gathering".

קוֹהֶלֶת (lit.) the "caller-out" or "summoner" (to a meeting). The name of the book of Ecclesiastes, or The Convener/Preacher. The form is the feminine of the *Qal* ptc; see **1da** and **2c** above. The feminine form, sometimes called the Feminine of Office, is another way of representing an occupation; cf. סוֹפֶרֶת "a (male) scribe", above. So Arabic *Caliphah*, the Caliph or ruler (of Baghdad).

קוֹל "voice, sound". Sixth Category. בַּת־קוֹל "echo" (lit., "daughter of a voice"). Modern Israel קוֹל־יִשְׂרָאֵל the National Broadcasting Authority.

קוּם "to arise". Hollow verb (II-*Waw*), see **3e** above; cf. the words of Jesus (Aramaic) טַלְיתָא קוּמִי "little lamb, get up" (Mark 5:41). See מָקוֹם above.

קָלַל "he was light (weight), insignificant". Geminate/doubled verb; stative. Cf. *Qal*, the first theme of the verb as "light, simple, unencumbered"; *Piel* (causative) קִלֵּל "he made light, contemptible, cursed".

קָנָה "he acquired, created". III-*He*/*lamed-he* verb.

קָרָא "he called; he read"; and followed by לְ "he named". III-*Aleph*/*lamed-aleph* verb; see **3ge** above. Cf. מִקְרָא as one of the Jewish designations for the Bible; also Arabic *Qurʾan* "what is called out" or "what is read", since reading is always out loud and public.

קֶרֶב "midst". Second Category (b) noun; cf. the frequent בְּקֶרֶב־ "in, in the middle of".

קֶרֶן "horn"; dual קַרְנַיִם. Second Category (a) noun.

Resh

רָאָה "he saw"; cf. רֹאֶה "Seer", and מַרְאֶה "sight, appearance". Fifth Category (a) nouns from III-*He*/*lamed-he* root.

רֹאשׁ "head"; plural רָאשִׁים. Sixth Category with quiescent *aleph*. On occasion a quiescent *aleph* attracts an "o" vowel, cf. the very common וַיֹּאמֶר. So in the singular, the quiescent *aleph* has an "o" vowel, but in the plural, the older "a" vowel is retained throughout; cf. Arabic *raʾs*.

רָבַב "he became many". Geminate/double *ayin* verb, related to the next entry.

רַב "great, great one, teacher". Fifth Category (b) noun, adjective; cf. רַבִּי "Rabbi; my teacher".

רָבָה "he increased, multiplied" (intransitive). III-*He*/*lamed-he* verb.

רֶגֶל "foot"; dual רַגְלַיִם. Second Category (a) noun; cf. Arabic *rajul* "man" (as walking).

רוּחַ "spirit, wind". Sixth Category noun fs. The furtive *patach* disappears when an ending is added to the word.

רוּם "to be high, exalted". Hollow verb (II-*Waw*); cf. the place Ramah רָמָה as "high".

רָחוֹק "far away, distant". First Category adjective.

רָחֵל "ewe"; Rachel.

רֶחֶם "womb". Second Category (a) noun.

רַחֲמִים "mercy, pity". The form indicates an associated abstract plural; cf. חַיִּים "life". Compare the titles of God in Exod. 34:6 רַחוּם, and of Allah in Arabic, *rachman* and *rachim* "merciful" and "compassionate".

רַע (m), רָעָה (f); –וֹת רָעִים (pl) "evil". Fifth Category (b) noun. Note the closed, short syllable רַע; when it becomes open by the addition of a second syllable the *patach* is lengthened to *qametz*.

רֵעַ and רֵעָה "friend, neighbour". Sixth Category and Fifth Category nouns, respectively.

רָפָא "he healed, repaired". The name רְפָאֵל a Levite (1 Chron. 26:7); cf. the angel of healing, *Raphael*; also 1 Kgs 18:30 speaks of Elijah "repairing" the altar.

רָשָׁע "wicked, evil" (person). First Category noun/adjective.

Sin

שָׂדֶה "field, open countryside". Fifth Category (a) noun. A common poetic variant in Old Hebrew retains the original *yod* שָׂדַי, cf. further **3da** above.

שִׂים "to put, place, set". Hollow verb (II-*Yod* with ◌ִי rather than וּ).

שִׂמְחָה "joy, gladness". Cf. the festival *Simchat-Torah* "the joy of the Torah/Law".

שָׂפָה "lip, language; coast" (as the "lip" of the sea). First Category fs noun.

שַׂר "prince, official"; שָׂרָה "princess"; cf. Sarah. Note all four nouns שַׂר, פַּר, צַר and מַר have a short, closed syllable in the masculine, but as soon as an ending is affixed the vowel under the first letter lengthens to ◌ָ, since it now comes in an open syllable. These words may be understood as First Category (technically they are "doublers", though in Masoretic Hebrew ר is not doubled, as once it was; cf. **1fb** above).

Shin

שָׁאַל "he asked". Cf. שָׁאוּל "asked for", i.e., the name Saul.

שְׁבִי "captivity". Fifth Category (a) noun.

שֶׁבַע "seven"; שָׁבוּעַ "a week" (seven days); cf. בְּאֵר־שֶׁבַע Beersheba.

שָׁבַר "he broke"; *Piel* שִׁבֵּר "he shattered".

שׁוּב "to return". Hollow verb (II-*Waw*). N.B. Isaiah's son שְׁאָר יָשׁוּב "A remnant shall return".

שִׁיר "song". Sixth Category. שִׁיר הַשִּׁירִים "The Song of Songs".

שָׁלוֹם "peace, well-being, wholeness". First Category noun. Proper name אַבְשָׁלוֹם Absalom. The formal greeting in Hebrew is שָׁלוֹם עֲלֵיכֶם "Peace be upon you"; cf. Luke 24:36. Its Arabic equivalent is *salaam ʿaleikum*. The formal greetings may be addressed to single persons as well as to a group. Modern Hebrew uses שָׁלוֹם for both "hello" and "good-bye".

שִׁלֵּם *Piel* "to pay, recompense (make wholeness)".

שָׁלַח "he sent"; cf. שִׁלֹחַ, i.e., the pool of Siloam (the Greek form of the name) as water "diverted, sent" (Isa. 8:6; John 9:7).

שֻׁלְחָן "table"; i.e., a mat, a rug, a piece of leather spread on the ground.

שֵׁם "name". Irregular, akin to Third Category noun, monosyllable. With suffixes the first syllable drops to *shewa*, e.g., שְׁמִי "my name", שְׁמוֹ "his name". With 2ms and 2fpl and 2mpl suffixes the first syllable has *hireq*, to avoid the forbidden two sounded *shewas*, e.g., שִׁמְךָ –כֶם, "thy/your name"; cf. בֵּן, above. The plural שֵׁמוֹת "names" is a (disguised) First Category noun. הַשֵּׁם is a reverential way of referring to God amongst Jews; בָּרוּךְ הַשֵּׁם "Blessed be the Name!", cf. English "thank goodness!".

שָׁמַיִם "heavens, sky" (apparently dual form, but in fact the *yod* is the third letter of the root). First Category noun.

שְׁמָמָה "destruction". First Category feminine noun.

שֶׁמֶן "(olive) oil". Second Category (a) noun. Cf. *Gethsemane* "olive press" (Matt. 26:36; Mk 14:32).

שָׁמַע "he heard". Cf. the *Shema*, the declaration of Jewish faith (Deut. 6:4-5).

שָׁמַר "he guarded, kept, watched"; cf. *Shomeron* "Samaria" (the "a" vowels of Samaria come from the Greek transliteration).

שֶׁמֶשׁ "sun". Cf. Arabic *shams* and the name Samson in Hebrew שִׁמְשׁוֹן; the "a" vowel of English derives from the Greek transliteration. It is possible that his hair (long and short) and the rays of the sun (strong and weak) are compared.

שֵׁן "tooth". Fifth Category (b). Root שׁנן.

שָׁנָה "year"; (pl) שָׁנִים. Root שׁנה "repeat"; cf. מִשְׁנָה *Mishnah* "what is repeated". שְׁנַיִם and שְׁתַּיִם (fem) "two". The *daghesh* represents the memory of the original *nun*.

שַׁעַר "(city) gate". Second Category (a) noun. The Orthodox quarter of Jerusalem is called מֵאָה שְׁעָרִים "hundred gates".

שָׁפַט "he judged". Participle שׁוֹפֵט "judge". Third Category. Cf. מִשְׁפָּט above.

שָׁתָה "he drank". III-*He*/*lamed-he* verb. Cf. מִשְׁתֶּה "feast, party".

Tav

תְּהִלָּה "praise, (song of) praise, psalm"; plural תְּהִלִּים (The Book of) Psalms; cf. הִלֵּל above.

תָּוֶךְ "middle". Fourth Category noun. Most used in the expression בְּתוֹךְ– "in the middle of".

תּוֹרָה "instruction, law, *Torah*"; also the Five Books of Moses. Sixth Category noun from root ירה "he cast, threw (i.e., the finger), he pointed the way".

תָּמִיד "continually, usually". Sixth Category adverb.

תָּמִים "perfect, complete". First Category adjective. The form is passive, and the collocation of vowels (◌ִי\◌ִ) often denotes status, or elsewhere appointment. Here the status is of a complete, perfect person.

תָּמַם "it was complete, finished". Geminate/doubled verb, see **3f** above.

תְּפִלָּה "prayer"; cf. הִתְפַּלֵּל above.